M000086164

BEING

HUMAN

NOW

BEING HUMAN NOW

Malu Wilder

Matthew Malu Wilder
Being Human Now
www.being-human-now.com

Dedicated to YOU
The Reader

You are a miracle, You are life itself

IMAGINE WHAT COULD HAPPEN IF WE
STOOD UP TOGETHER IN TRUST
AND FULLY ACKNOWLEDGED
THAT THIS WORLD BELONGS TO US

About The Movement

The Being Human Now movement is comprised of individuals working in unity to create change using direct and peaceful action in their daily lives.

Through protest organization, unified product boycotts, changes in social architecture and daily acts of courageous vulnerability; people working within the BHN network are organizing to actively create a better tomorrow. Each of us are working in our own way, bringing what we can: honestly as ourselves.

By working in unity we ARE capable of enacting real change. The tide of misogyny, racism and environmental destruction can be turned when we act together as one.

A better world is possible.

The time is now, and we are the ones we have been waiting for.

The BHN Network can be found here:

http://www.being-human-now.com/network

Table of Contents

Forward

Chapter 1 Being Human Now

Chapter 2 Reclaiming The Body: The Birthright Of The Senses

Chapter 3 The Inner Call To Action

Chapter 4 Hero's Call

Chapter 5 Relative Reality

Chapter 6 It Might Just Be A Renaissance

Chapter 7 The Power Of True Presence

Chapter 8 Chasing The Carrot

Chapter 9 Flipping The Coin Of The Inner Monologue

Chapter 10 Synchronizing The Inner And Outer Experience

Chapter 11 Being Seen And Holding Space

Chapter 12 Direct Experience: Breaking the Chains Of Conceptual Illusion

Chapter 13 Unipolar Thinking And The Myth Of Opposites

Chapter 14 Painting With The Same Colors

Chapter 15 Courageous Vulnerability

Chapter 16 The Great Myth of Sexual Purity: Unashamed To Be Human, Unashamed To Have Needs

Chapter 17 Personal Revolution and Gentle Bravery

Chapter 18 Collective Awakening

Chapter 19 Spiritual Ninjutusu And Radical Interdependence

You are so much more

than

you think you are....

FORWARD

ༀ་མ་ཎི་པདྨེ་ཧཱུྃ

There is a realization readily available to all of us; a truth sitting right under our noses. There is a secret hidden in such plain sight that it is easy to live the span of an entire life without ever seeing it. You have been lied to by the powers that be. But you already know that. There is something not quite right about the way we have been taught to interact with each other, about the way have been taught to interact with ourselves. There is a very subtle sensation that something is off with the way we have been taught to view the world. It's almost all there.... but something is missing, something isn't right.

I believe I have discovered the subtle ways that we have been lied to, and how our greatest power has been hidden from us. The powers that be have done this much more from a state of confusion and fear than malicious intention. There isn't really one enemy at all. The battle between freedom and repression is happening inside all of us every single day. There is no single terrible human at the core of it all. However, there are many who are using cognitive tools en mass to repress us.

The targeted repression of self and mind is occurring, pushed on us by the systemic and conceptual powers that be. Through a carefully constructed and incredibly subtle set of cognitive programming, we have been convinced that we are powerless. Or rather, our true power has been hidden behind a deep wall of shame and systemically programmed guilt. Fed to us bit by bit by the systems in place, as if they had any claim to it at all.

We have been trained to be afraid of what we actually are, in our completeness. We have been convinced that change can occur only by obeying the rules, or breaking them lightly. Rules that have been put in place to create a "safe" society. A society that has proven to be anything but safe. These rules may do a lot of good in many ways, and are even necessary to some degree, but they must be seen as secondary to life not as the end all be all of truth.

I feel the need now to blow the lid off of this lie, and point directly to your power. Because I believe I have begun to find where that power truly lies in each of us. I believe I have begun to see how it has been hidden from us. Our power lies in all the places that we least expect it, along with the several that we do see clearly. If you bare with me I will try to show you the tip of this iceberg, however massive of a truth it may be. I can not show you all of it at once, but I can begin to tell you the truth that I have found.

It has been said that they who claim enlightenment are not enlightened. While this has been true for the vast majority of the current paradigm, it is beginning to change to some degree. Enlightenment is a never-ending process with no true end goal, however the world today requires pointing directly at the truth to get people to listen at all. People demand spoilers before they are even willing to be interested, and while this is unfortunate, it is also understandable given the massive influx of information we are faced with every day. In a way, this demand for spoilers is sane. We have to filter what is thrown at us somehow.

And so, I am going to give you a spoiler. In the following pages you will be pointed towards what is referred to in many eastern philosophical and spiritual traditions as enlightenment. You will be pointed to a direct and easy path. A path that is available without religion, without dogma and without any oppression of what you are. The truth is I am not really supposed to tell you that.

I'm not really supposed to tell you any of this at all. According to the spiritual powers that be, you are supposed to be left to figure it out yourself. However, it has become obvious that the time is now and we are the ones we have been waiting for. The powers that be are not going to save us and neither are their rules. This is on us as the youth minds of the world. That's all there is to it.

There are many in the mystical and wisdom based spiritual communities that may be upset at how direct this manuscript is. They will say that people are meant to sit and meditate and figure this stuff out themselves. They will say true Dharma is taught only by hinting at the truth. They will say that pointing directly to the truth as I am about to do is vulgar in a way, and should be a task saved for the "masters", the old teachers. They will say you need one particular teacher, one particular source.

There are many in the greater spiritual communities of the world who will cling to their lineages, cling to their books, cling to their teachings without ever cracking the egg of their religions and finding the truth inside. Their own personal and sacred truth, beyond religion. They are doomed to worship the packaging around the truth, without ever opening the gift that has been given to them. They are doomed to worship symbols instead of meaning. They are likely to sit in their meditation halls, to sit in their churches and temples and continue to preach while the world burns down. They are likely to preach compassion but walk by a starving homeless man on the street without a second look. They are likely to use the teachings of truth and compassion only to further their own positions in the world.

To those who would stand in the way of progress and change, know that your's is a fool's errand. The new generation is here and we are not defined by age, race, gender or creed. We are simply defined by the knowledge that things could be better, that freedom from the old ways and conceptual constructs is now of vital importance. We are defined by a willingness to take our own power, without allowing anyone else to dictate it to us. We are defined by a respect for the past that does not demoralize our future. You may fear our embrace of new forms of sexuality, you may fear the end to misogyny and the embrace of the powerful feminine aspect, you may fear our advancement of technology, you may fear our dedication to environmental sustainability, you may fear our willingness to operate based upon our own knowledge and inner compass, you may fear our freedom of thought and expression. You may fear us, but you cannot stop us. The chains of religiously and conceptually induced shame cannot touch us. For we are one and we are many, we are the future and we are the truth. Through nonviolent and radical dedication, change is coming. The new generation is here. Change is HERE. Let go or be dragged.

The internal overthrowing of our conceptual prison, the internal acceptance of true power is what they fear the most. So let's do it. Let's change the world and see what happens. Let us embrace our deepest selves without the dogmas of the past. Let's fall in love with the moment, and in so doing create an actual future.

A lot of the information I am about to share with you is present in Buddhist "root texts." These are texts that are at the core of Buddhist teachings and are often hidden from the public eye either in plain sight or behind closed doors. It is said that normal people like you and I could "never understand them, and thus we should not have free access to them." To some degree this is true, because they were written thousands of years ago and the context shift to today's view can be difficult to grasp without a translator. Some of the people who would say that wisdom should be hidden would do this out of a sense of compassion and skill. The truth is that if you are told too much too quickly, it is likely that you will shut down. That you may not be able to actually process what is being said to you.

However it seems that too many people who are willing to keep wisdom hidden do it out of ego. They do it out of a sense of fear. They hold teachings as badges of honor and thus lose the truth. Too many are the people who are content to ride the high holy horse of spiritual hierarchy while the world goes to shit around them. I think you deserve to know the truth, to discover and be given it, to take it and throw it away as you see fit. I trust my reader, I trust that my reader is the truth, and in that I find the freedom to tell you what I have found.

It is incredibly important to remember as you read this that there is no true enemy outside of ourselves. The illusion of an external enemy is a very useful one, it bands people together, it inspires them to get to work. It gives us a target for our inspiration, someone to overthrow. It has been used by leaders and people working in the background throughout history. The illusion of an enemy is very powerful. So I will use it here. I will make reference to them and they who are controlling you, and in a way this is appropriate. In a way this is true. There are powerful people who are purposefully controlling the world via cognitive programming. But the honest truth is that even the most evil and cruel seeming people are suffering greatly as well. They are, more than anyone else, slaves to the old paradigm and they are terrified of you realizing what I am about to tell you in this book. They are not really the enemy, they are more like zombies or a brain washed army. They can wake up too. They are sacred and vital life force just like any of the rest of us. They are part of the pattern of existence and in their own way, they are beautiful. There is no such thing as evil.

Understand that there certainly is something to

overthrow. There is a direct and obvious way of thinking to rally against, this is not a vague concept. There is an enemy, but that enemy is not one person or group of people. It is the overall confusion that humanity is currently presented with, and we are going to need to regard it as a friend if we are going to change it.

Some people are awake and some people are not, and that distinction does not seem to have anything to do with a particular spiritual, conceptual or political hierarchy. That "awake" quality is just not represented by one person or set of beliefs. At this point in our history the only true enemy is a conceptual one. A mess of cognitive training and lies that has been passed down through the generations. Truth and confusion are present in all of us, side by side.

As we dive into these concepts together it is important to understand that this is a path, not a destination. This idea of enlightenment or personal evolution cannot be fully captured by any one book or explanation. It cannot be held down at all. It is not one thing, and yet it is. It is purposefully left open, that is part of its nature. But in the following pages, I intend to point you to the tip of the iceberg. I intend to help demystify and make more easily available the beginnings of enlightenment or the evolution of consciousness. Call it what you will.

This is a far simpler thing than we imagine, and it is more a matter of seeing through the illusion that has been presented to you throughout your life. The process of conscious evolution has been thoroughly blocked up by the spiritual and conceptual hierarchies of the world. They have all but stolen true spirituality from us, each one trying to claim it as their own. Trying to claim you as their own. You are their battleground and their commodity, the field of your mind.

It is of vital importance to remember that the truths presented here must be experienced, they cannot just be read about if you wish to understand them. For they are your truths and they are my truths. They are simple truths akin to the truth of a sun rise. They are some of the core truths of being human. In the following pages I am going to attempt to tell you some of the hidden truth. It may at first glance not seem very hidden. A lot of it will seem obvious to some degree. However it you look closely, you will see the core deception that we have been presented with, and then the truth will begin to become clear. The antidote is in the poison. This book is an attempt to begin to show you something incredibly profound, and if you really look you will start to see it.

If this information does not serve you, then please throw it away as fast as possible. This book could be of incredible help to some, but if it does not help you then I hope you throw it in your fireplace. That would be of more help to your freedom of mind than any book. The world now needs to become our teacher, and there are many sources of wisdom. The only question is, are you listening? I have already told you several secrets in this introduction that you probably didn't even notice...

They have robbed you of your senses, robbed you of the basic joys of existence, confused the inner compass, convinced us to hate ourselves, and left us with quite a terrible mess in the world. But there is no one to hate, and in fact hate is at the core of the illusion. This was done to you out of fear and a lack of understanding.

They never meant to victimize you, or if they did they were not fully aware of the reasons why. They were simply passing down what they knew, as confused as much of it may be.

We are all in this together. They have tried to steal our personal and fundamental power as human beings, however things are changing and the wall is crumbling. People ARE beginning to wake up, and now is the time to ride the wave.

It is with deep love and a profound respect for your noble and beautiful individual experience that I present to you the following work. I do hope that it serves you on your path to personal freedom. If it doesn't then I hope you throw it in the mud.

Chapter One:

Being Human Now

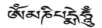

It is a fantastic and terrifying time to be alive. We wake every day to news of vast technological advancements in every sphere. The study and practice of modern medicine is pushing the idea of human health and potential to new heights, with new treatments and cures for disease and injury being discovered at an ever increasing pace. The study of our environment and the natural laws that govern

1

it is leading to discoveries about the base nature of matter and existence itself that even the most powerful minds alive are struggling to fully grasp the meaning of.

We are more connected than ever before, constantly sharing ideas, knowledge and wisdom on a global scale that was hardly imaginable even twenty years ago. Through the internet, global networking, and the smartphone revolution we are building a global mind, a global experience. Any and all possible human experience and knowledge is being recorded, shared, and compared by video, text, chat and e-mail. Discoveries in one person's mind, laboratory, classroom or business can be shared with another across the world in less than a second. A global processing of data is occurring at a rapid rate that is making way for discoveries that we can hardly even dream of. It seems as if we are in a new renaissance, witnessing and taking part in the awakening of a connected and networked world.

Simultaneously, alongside all of these fantastic achievements, we are bearing witness to one of the most frightening times on earth. We are surrounded by constant conversation and evidence of our potentially looming destruction. At times it seems that the light of this new revolution serves mainly to show us our darkest side as a species. The ozone is in a state of degradation, the ice caps are melting as the seas are rising, and the world is heating up. Vast quantities of water are becoming poisoned and unusable, the oceans are tainted with pollution of all kinds. The biodiversity of our planet is shrinking as different species of animals and plants are pushed to extinction. There is an area of plastic garbage in the pacific ocean larger than the state of Texas where nothing lives, not even plankton, and it is growing larger every day.

We are constantly bombarded with the possibility of war, or a school shooting, or a terrorist act. The darkest parts of our society are now coming into the light. The base shadow of racism and misogyny that has plagued us for so long is rearing its ugly head and adding it's voice to the global mind. We are seeing all of the dark, and the light come into the open, naked and true.

It is a difficult and yet wonderful time to be alive. History is being made every day and in every way imaginable. We are pushing forward together as a species and having to look deeply at everything that has held us back, everything that truly threatens our survival. We are questioning, learning and defining together what it really means to be human, what it really means to be alive. This time is not easy, it can feel crushing and terrifying just to get out of bed in the morning. But there is also excitement, there is also hope for what we could become together.

I believe that as frightening as the world can seem these days, we also have absolutely everything we need to fix it. I believe that we are in the beginnings of a revolution, the revolution of self. We are entering a time that will demand that we show up, exactly as we are, offering exactly what we each have to give. I believe that we can create a world of justice, gentleness and respect. A world that honors the beauty and potential of human life. I believe we can transform this world into a far more sane place to live. I believe we can do it starting now, right here, on the spot. But only if we are able to collectively look inside and truly offer whatever it is we have to give to this world, however we can help to transform it. We can all become heroes in our own right, if we are willing to stand up exactly as we are.

The intention of this book, and all of my writing, is to contribute what I can to the current rise of human evolution. The following pages contain a perspective on modern life which is derived from a combination of my life experiences and discoveries as a scholar and practitioner of eastern philosophies and spiritual modalities. Through this study I believe that I have found several concepts, ideas and life practices that can be of great value to all us that are challenged with the daily act of being human now. This book is only an introduction, there is so much more to come.

It is my greatest wish that these findings may be of some benefit to others on this journey of modern life. Before we are anything else, we are all human and we are all in this together. Whether we like it or not.

CHAPTER TWO:

RECLAIMING THE BODY: THE BIRTHRIGHT OF THE SENSES

ཨོཾ་མ་ཎི་པདྨེ་ཧཱུྃ

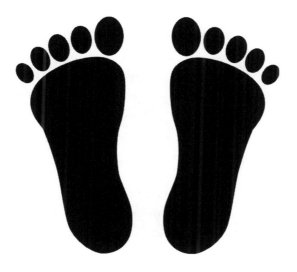

We were born to experience, to feel the world around us. Our entire physical make up revolves around our senses, our brains are deeply wired to receive and respond to stimulus. Our ability to feel fulfilled and happy is deeply tied to the senses. Our very survival as a species

5

has relied on our ability to sense, relate to and then respond to the outside world. In fact our entire physical makeup is built to support our senses. In every possible way we are made to feel deeply.

We have such an endless amount of experience at our finger tips in this modern world, so much to see, taste, smell, hear and feel. Yet it seems that people are more and more likely to shut down, shut in, and rely on the very small world of their phones, computers and homes to define most of what they are able to experience. There is a quality of openness to our surroundings, a presence with each other and acceptance of ourselves that seems to be less and less popular. It seems that while the global world is becoming more connected, our actual experience of life is becoming smaller and smaller, more restricted to our screens and daily habits.

In pointing this out, I do not mean at all to be judgmental. In fact if this tendency of closing in is looked at on a social-emotional level, it makes perfect sense. We are constantly bombarded with random demands on our attention and focus. All of the inter-connectivity has, as a side effect, created a situation where we feel less and less able to be here. We are expected to be at attention and ready to respond almost all of the time. There is always someone else's life to look at on social media, some major piece of news breaking, a meeting or a phone call, a text or an email. There is always something.

On top of it, a lot of what we are constantly bombarded with is negative and fear inducing. We are practically

6

forced to be exposed to terrifying and depressing news and tendencies in people every day. It hurts. It makes us want to close down, to pull the blankets over our heads, pop our earbuds in, and hide. It doesn't help that at our finger tips we have all of the distraction necessary to hide away and pretend none of it is happening for the rest of our lives. It is now easier than ever to make a perfect little box to live in, shrinking our experiences down to only the ones we select and control.

As wonderful as it can be to make our own little oasis, as helpful as it can be to have a safe place to fall back to, it is also so easy to over do. We become less and less likely to allow new experience in, we begin to refuse to see and experience the world exactly as it is, right here right now. Our worlds become an echo chamber, things become trite and sour. As our chosen worlds begin to bore us, we are faced with the option of chasing a new set of distractions or simply giving in further and becoming depressed. The rhythm of a purely habitual life may bore us, it may depress us, but at least it feels safe and familiar. So we can easily sink in even more deeply. We can easily get lost in a world of our own habitual thoughts and projections. In an effort to avoid pain and fear, we end up feeling less and less of everything. We can even feel less alive.

I mean think about it, really think about it. How normal is it for someone to break eye contact with you and check their phones mid conversation? How normal is it for you to do the same? How often are we actually aware of our surroundings anymore, actually engaged and present in the current time and space we are in? When was the last time you felt your entire body, were just simply aware of it?

Try this right now, right where you are. Become aware of the sensation of the clothing you are wearing, every little stitch. Feel the weight of your shirt, the snugness of your socks. Feel your feet on the ground or your sit bones in the chair. Become aware of the temperature of the air in the room, feel it on your skin. Invite every centimeter of your body to give you information. Put the book, or kindle, or phone, or computer down. Sit with that for a moment, just feel what it is like to actually be you, right here, right now. Maybe notice the brightest color in the room, take it in and appreciate it for however it makes you feel. I humbly request that you take a moment to do this right now. Not a long time, just a moment.

Did you do it?

If you did you may have noticed my point: we just aren't actually here very often. We are pulled away by thought of something else, somewhere else. We plan what we will do when we get out of work tonight, and by the time we get there we are already thinking of the next day of work. Arriving at work again the next day we begin to plan what we will do when we are free for the evening.

We do this in smaller ways too. Looking forward to the next minute, the next hour, the next five minutes. Planning and planning, but not even being with the act of planning itself. It's almost as if we are constantly waiting for something to happen, and even as that thing happens we are already onto the next thing. At some point it's probably worth stopping and asking ourselves "Wait a second, what the fuck am I waiting for?"

This is honestly very sad, it's a huge loss on our parts. The world around us is actually quite beautiful. It is full of bright and wonderful colors, incredible flavors, sunrises, surprise encounters with friends, glimpses of humanity in people's eyes.... We move through these experiences, but most of the time we don't really let them in. There is such an incredible amount of life to live and experience to have, a depth of being human, that is available in every moment. All we have to do is check in. Come here now. Feel what we are actually feeling, be honest with ourselves and let it all in. We can do this on both a sensory level, and an emotional level.

The key is to understand that emotion is a spectrum and

depression shrinks that spectrum. If we want to experience all of the beauty and depth that life has to offer, we have to be willing to feel all of it. Joy defines sadness and sadness defines joy. We don't get to choose what not to feel, you either feel more or you feel less, and in the end you always feel no matter what. We are just simply built for it.

So the more we let it all in, the more oriented to the truth of reality we become. Sure it's not necessarily all good or always what we want, but it is real. Being human is not a science, it's an art. It requires all of the depth and dynamism that it offers to actually function. Being human is not done on a straight line, it is done in all of the jagged dips and turns and spirals that are present in complex art. Living this life artfully requires a certain degree of surrender to the moment. It can't be perfectly planned and executed, that simply is not how it works. It is messy, and in that mess lies the beauty of it all. In that mess lies the true grace and gentle power of it all.

So where do we start? We start right where we are, right here, right now, over and over again. That means checking in with the senses, with the way the world makes us feel. It means purposefully remembering to look deeply, to hear, to see and smell. It means being awake, on purpose. It means taking a moment whenever we remember, to feel the clothes on our backs and the air on our faces. It means that instead of zoning out, we zone in. We allow the current sensory input to touch us deeply, we allow it to make visceral contact with us. In this way we can begin to

10

touch our true power in the moment. A power that has been hidden from us.

When we listen to someone speak, we can allow their voices to affect us the way music does. We can feel them in our bodies. When we see a bright color or contrast of colors in our daily lives, we can appreciate them the way we would art in a fine museum. When we walk we can feel the pressure of the ground on our feet and appreciate the feeling of wearing shoes. We can see raw beauty in the clouds and take the time to show up, right here, right now. This idea sounds so straight forward, but it is the key to experiencing the raw edge of reality.

There is a simple and yet very dynamic meditation practice we can use to train our minds to return to and be aware of our more subtle sensations. It is a very old practice and here I will call it a "Body Scan Release".

This practice is all about coming into full contact with what it feels like to be in your own body, and then using the body focused opportunity to release any ambient and residual tension. The practice is done in two parts, one on the inhale and one on the exhale. We begin by closing our eyes and focusing on one part of the body. As we breathe in, we feel that part of the body completely and imagine that we are breathing in through it. We then use the exhale to release any tension that we have found, and after a few breaths like this, we move on to another part of the body. The idea is to use the combined focus on body sensation and the breath, together, to release stuck and tense feelings.

11

Here is an example:

Sitting comfortably, bring your attention to the top of
your head and breathe in. As you inhale, simply feel
everything that you can in your scalp and the top of your
head. Allow the breath to combine with any sense of
tension or heaviness that you find in your scalp. You can
imagine that the breath is mingling with and combining
with the sensation of tension, or you can imagine that the
breath soaks up the tension like a sponge, or even that the
breath creates a container for, and holds the tension. The
important thing is that we are breathing directly into any
tension that we feel and allowing the breath to become
one with it. As we breathe out, the tension rides out with
breath, leaving behind a more relaxed feeling in the top of
the head.

Do this for three to five breaths while focusing on the
top of the head, and then move down to the forehead.
Focus on the sensation in your forehead, your temples, the
sides of your head and the back of your head. Everywhere
a headband would sit. Again, breathe in and feel
everything you can in this part of the head. Just allow it to
tell you about any sensations that are present there. When
and if you find any tension, breathe directly into it and
soak it up with the breath. Combine the feeling of the
tension with the feeling of breathing in. As you exhale,
allow the tension or heaviness to simply ride out with the
breath. This feels a lot like a sigh, it has the same sense of

12

release on the breath. Again, continue focusing on the forehead and temples for three to five breaths and then move your attention down to the eye sockets, cheekbones and jaw.

Continue down through your entire body, the neck and shoulders, chest and heart, arms and hands, stomach, hips, legs and feet. Each time, applying this feeling of breathing into any tension you find, combining the breath with it, and breathing it out fully as if with a sigh. As you move through your hands and feet, pay special attention to extending your mind into each finger and toe. Just see what they feel like, explore the sensation entirely.

If you come across a particularly heavy or stuck feeling point, it can be useful to use a visualization of an opening spiral. Imagine a spiral opening in the tense part of the body as you breathe out.

You can use a visualization of a camera iris, or an opening flower, or any thing else that spirals open. So let's say you find a lot tension in the palms of your hands, you can imagine an opening flower or camera iris in the palms of your hands as you breathe out. The opening spiral visualization tends to be very effective at triggering the release of muscle tension, particularly when combined with an exhale.

The body scan release practice can be done on the entire body, or for much shorter amounts of time on particular parts of the body. It is perfectly fine to do a scan on one particular sore or tense part of your body if you don't feel you have time to do the full meditation.

The habit of checking in with our more subtle sensations becomes quite natural quite quickly when we practice it. This is because it is our birthright, it is the birthright of the senses. Above all else, this body is yours. No one can tell you how to use it or what to experience with it. So long is it brings no harm to another life, it is our prerogative as human beings to live. To feel deeply, here and now.

CHAPTER THREE:

THE INNER CALL TO ACTION

ༀ་མ་ཎི་པ་དྨེ་ཧཱུྃ

Waking to this world every day has a tendency to create what can feel like completely opposing emotions in us. We are at once aware of the excitement and potential available in today's current world, we know that if we want to we can actually get up and do something, something worthwhile. People, knowledge, travel and experiences of all kinds are at our fingertips. We can study anything, find entertainment in a myriad of ways and have access to food from all over the world. In the west, even without realizing it we live like queens and kings of old as far as resources are concerned.

But then we feel the dread, the fear. That little bit of extra anxiety that seems to pop up throughout the day. The ever looming truth of possible loss, the sadness at the destruction of our planet, the fear that it could all just end *snap, just like that. Even on a mundane level we are surrounded by what can feel like overwhelming demands for our attention and time. Constant news feeds, social media, connection with acquaintances, our jobs and our debts, our family dramas. It can at times all feel so lumped on top of itself that it seems almost impossible to push our way out.

If we are to find our way forward individually and as a global society, we must find ways to allow the inspiration that we feel to be our primary focus. It is a great challenge to be aware of all that is terrifying and painful about the world. But as we learn to focus on that inner voice of excitement and inspiration, it can become a wonderful story to live every single day. We feel challenge, we feel fear, we feel sadness and we let it hit us, we let it in. We accept it as the trigger for our best qualities of fearlessness and an ability to create happiness in our lives. We let the tenderness of the pain strike us deeply, but instead of falling backwards we allow it to make us smile, we allow it to inspire us towards change.

By sitting fully with our inner experience, we can use

16

fear to create bravery and sadness to create tenderness and care. We can harness these parts of ourselves that feel so terrible and alien. The parts we have been trained to ignore. From this way of viewing things, our most difficult feelings can become the best internal catalyst for change. For it is the act of showing up against terrible odds, no matter what, that ties all stories of heroism together.

You see the biggest lie they have told us, the most blatant way they have hidden our power from us, is by telling us that we have to run from any part of ourselves at all, that we have to fix some fundamental failure in ourselves. This is very deeply ingrained in us as a society and people, this feeling that we are somehow broken and must be fixed. This idea that there are parts of ourselves that are disgusting or terrible, parts of ourselves that we cannot learn to embrace and love. They have tried to tell you that doing so would result in a loss of control, that you would turn into some over emotional savage. But this simply is not true. They have lied to you because they are lying to themselves.

Our power lies in our completeness as individuals and a society. Our power lies in every single part of us. Our true and complete power lies in all the dark parts, the light parts and all the parts in between. Every single aspect of our experience can be equally respected. When we actually try to stop running from what we are feeling, we become less fragmented and begin to find who we truly are. We become more oriented to reality the way it actually is. With this awareness and acceptance, we can access a skill and art of living life that is missed by most people.

Bravery, true bravery is the ability to show up, unashamed of who we are, fully, and honestly non aggressive towards the world around us. Now THAT is difficult. But when we are able to do it, when we are able to show up right here, right now exactly as we are and completely unashamed... Well then we are free. We find that it is actually a totally natural state of being, and life gains a whole new depth, a whole new purpose. How much can I be right here, right now, honestly human, honestly myself? How much can I do that in a way that helps the people and world around me, or at least does not harm it? Everyday becomes a game of sorts, a light hearted attempt to handle ourselves and the world around us with an active and engaged, yet gentle touch.

Along with freedom, we find incredible and immense personal power. We find that there has been a part of us, a large portion of our energy and effort, tied up in running from and disliking ourselves. It's not that we become more powerful, more that we take hold of the power that we have always had. We free it up by becoming totally ok with what we are, and in that we find great power to change the world around us, and make our dreams come true. Slowly but surely, by practicing just actually showing up on the spot we become simultaneously more gentle and more effective in very surprising ways.

This can be done by challenging ourselves to sit with the thoughts and feelings that make us want to run. We can show our face to the sides of ourselves that we don't like, the parts that scare us. When we do, they often begin to melt away. When we sit through the anxiety without picking up our phones, when we feel uncomfortable and don't immediately try to distract ourselves, when we choose to relax and lean into it instead... we find ourselves, right here and now. We find the part of ourselves that we have been subtly hiding from for our entire lives. We find our truth.

There is a direct meditative practice that can help us immensely in this process of sitting with, and accepting, exactly what we are. One of the fastest ways we can begin to shed mental programing and clear the loud clutter from our minds is through a practice I like to call "mental de-fragmentation". Through this practice, we address, process and release the residual thoughts and emotional

19

clutter that gathers throughout our lives and our days. All of the little bits of stress, anxiety, sadness, anger, and over excitement that gather up throughout a day can be released in a relatively short period of time using this practice.

Doing this with a certain degree of regularity will also begin to give you some insight into the subtle programing that has been taught to us throughout our lives. This practice is one of the most direct and accessible ways that we can begin to release stuck patterns of habitual thought and emotion, allowing us to move into a more spontaneous and authentic experience of life.

Sit somewhere in a comfortable position that you can hold for around ten minutes. It is best to sit with your back upright, or to choose a position to sit in "on purpose". Focus your mind on your breath. Feel each part of the process of breathing. The breath into and out of your nose and your throat, the expansion and contraction of your chest, and stomach, and diaphragm as you breathe in and out. Feel simply what it is like to be you, sitting right there on the spot and breathing. As other thoughts come to your mind, notice them gently and say to yourself in your mind "that's ok". See and feel the thought that comes up, and simply label with a true and deep feeling of "that's totally ok". Once you have labeled the thought, return your attention to your breath and try to breathe the thought out. Release it with the feeling of "that's ok" and bring your attention back to the breath. Just returning to the full feeling of being you, breathing, right there, right now, on

20

the spot.

The real trick with this practice is that we label every single thought in the same way, no matter what it is. Both pleasant thoughts and scary ones, thoughts of the future and thoughts of the past, even gruesome or violent thoughts are all met with this deep sense of "that's ok" and then released out with the breath. As we return our minds to the breath, we let go of any residual thought that may be left. It is important to note that we are not justifying any action with this practice, we are simply noticing a thought as a thought and nothing more. We are not saying to ourselves that "it's ok" to do anything, we are saying it's ok to think anything. They are just thoughts.

If you become distracted at all throughout the process, don't worry about it. When you notice you are distracted, use the "that's ok" label for whatever you find yourself thinking about, and return your attention to the breath.

On a cognitive level, the effect of this practice can be incredibly profound. Essentially what we are doing is sifting through the active contents of our minds and mentally "checking things off" as we go. Thought by thought, we give ourselves total permission to let go of the residual emotions and mental clutter that gather throughout a day.

Doing this practice daily for five to ten minutes can yield incredible results. Over time you will notice how much extra weight and background noise we tend to carry in our minds. You will also begin to uncover, layer by layer, the deepest aspects of your own cognitive processing. You

will begin to more fully experience the forming of
thought, and better understand the functioning of your
mind on a very personal level.

Chapter Four:

A CALL TO HEROES

ༀ་ཏུ་རི་ཨཱཿ་རི་ཏུ་རི་སྭཱ་ཧཱ

We are alive at an honest and real crossroads of human evolution. The future of our earth, the future of our social systems, and the future of humankind is quite literally in our hands. Evolution or annihilation, it may sound dramatic but that is the current truth. The next twenty to thirty years of our history will dramatically define our future as a species.

For some people, this idea is too overwhelming. It shuts them down, and they fall back on philosophical or intellectual defenses. Claiming that they cannot help the world around them, or that there are no real problems, or calling those who do stand egotistical and crazy. But for some people this idea is a source of great inspiration. For some of us, the idea that the world needs us now wakes us up. It gives us energy to stand up and act.

Some of you who read this will understand it on a deeper level immediately. I know you are out there. I know you can feel it too. This call that the time is coming, the time is here. The time to open, to stand up internally exactly as we are, in our strength. That the time to give what we can is nearing, the time to allow our hidden gifts to shine is now.

I know you are out there, feeling this hero's call. I know we are waking up together. I know that you may have been keeping your light a secret. To some very large degree, you may feel powerless and alone.

I am here to tell you that in a very real way, you are not alone. There are many of us rising, many of us accepting truth beyond conceptual imprisonment. Truth beyond borders, truth beyond the failed status quo. Truth without violence or repression. There are many of us dedicated to the actuality of a better future.

We may not be the heroes that the world expected. We may not fit into some particular mold or example. We don't always look like the heroes of the movies. We are probably more ragtag and mixed than anyone would have guessed. We may be from different countries, different walks of life, and different expressions of self altogether.

We probably aren't the heroes that the world thought it was waiting for, but we are the heroes that it has. We are the heroes that it needs. We are alive now in a time of great change, great opportunity and great difficulty. We have access to resources beyond historical measure, we can actually make a difference now, right where we stand. We are currently aligned in a way that no other group of people has ever been aligned before. We are alive in a time of great desperation, yet we have access to great strength, wisdom and abilities.

If you are feeling this call then I ask you, why wouldn't we now take on our deepest gifts and allow the universe to act through us? The only reason I can see is that we don't believe in our own power, we are afraid of our own potential. There is no limit here, nothing holding us back. It is only our beliefs and our habitual patterns that prevent us from claiming our birthright, that prevent us from bowing our heads to the universe and standing internally as heroes now. Nothing existed until it did, no human invention or vision ever came to life until someone pushed it forward.

By heroes I do not mean some caped fighter of crime. In fact a true hero is entirely non violent. A true hero can be found in any crowd and any life situation. A true hero works with the reality in front of them, engaging with the world in the most productive and loving possible manner. Non violence is the way, we must work within society gently and tirelessly if we are to make real change.

When it comes to expressing joy and love on earth, when it comes to expressing the height of humanity: the highest levels of intellect, patience, compassion, presence, skill and virtue. When it comes to expressing the absolute best of humankind: We are IT. Right now.

If we aren't embodying the best that humankind has to offer in our own personal way, we can't be sure that it's being embodied anywhere. Simply by nature of being alive at this time, we are what the world has to work with. There is a power in that, a power that we should not ignore. What happens from here is quite directly, up to us.

Creating real and sustainable positive change is a simple matter of believing in ourselves and taking responsibility for the world around us as much as we can. It means keeping ourselves safe and strong, while engaging directly with the problems in the world. The problems in our neighborhoods, the problems in our cities, in our states, in our countries and in global society as a whole. There are many who are not ready to hear this call, and that is OK. There are currently more than enough of us showing up. If you are hearing this call, then the world needs you. The time is now.

This means engaging directly with the systems in place, in the ways that we have access to, each in our own right. It means supporting one another in a shared vision for a cleaner, less violent, safer, more expressive, more artistic, more sustainable, fair and justice oriented world. It means showing up in our daily lives carrying this light. It means being willing to walk into the wind and rain face first, fully accepting the storm. Walking through the torrent until we find the sun.

If we are able to wake up every day making the decision that today we will embody the very best version of humanity that we can, then we have purpose. Understand that you are human evolution, right here and now. If we wake with that commitment, then it doesn't matter where we are in our lives, we can make a very real positive difference. We could be working in a coffee shop, or we could be a CEO, we could be young or we could be old, rich or poor. We could write a book, or volunteer in our neighborhoods or work for social justice and change via government and protesting. We could invent the next amazing green technology... It doesn't matter where we are in life. If we wake every day with the intention to be the best that humanity has to offer right where we are, in our own shoes, then we are contributing to a saner and more evolved world. If enough of us do this, then we will automatically create that world together. If we want to live in a better world, then we have to be willing to make one. No one else is going to do it for us.

This means that every time we hear that inner call to inspired and gentle action, we follow it. Pick up that trash on the street, show up for your family and friends, follow your inspiration and write that book or dance or paint, volunteer to help struggling parts of your community, direct your art towards radical change, if you have resources then donate them to a higher and actionable cause, if you don't have resources then donate your time. Most importantly, decide very clearly that you desire to represent pure compassionate action on earth, and allow that to guide everything that you do. Do exactly what you can, gently and powerfully, right now.

We need to be working on ourselves and fully showing up for one another. If the creation of a better tomorrow is going to continue to fall on the shoulders of those who choose to show up, then we are going to need to be willing to hold each other up and inspire one another. We are going to need to connect and to network, to share resources, ideas, time and emotional support. No single one of us can take on the problems of the world alone.

For this reason, in the front and back of this book you will find a link to the central hub of a growing network. This page will direct you to ongoing discussions, groups and coordinated action based efforts between people of all walks of life. People who are dedicated to a greener, more sustainable, more creative, more compassionate and finally more equal future for all of humankind. People who are willing to act from inspired and powerful, yet gentle action. If you are hearing this call, please feel free to join in this ongoing discussion and coordination.

There is a global awakening happening. It is happening in every city, in every town, and in every country. It is non violent and gentle, but it is not afraid. If you don't want to see it, then you won't. If you aren't willing to stand up and join this growing dedication to a better world, then it simply won't present itself to you. It cannot be pinpointed exactly, because it is happening inside of us as individuals all over the world.

However, to those of us that do feel this call, to those of us who are willing to be with their power and dedicate themselves to positive change: I want you to know very clearly that you are not alone.

We each have latent gifts and abilities that the world now needs. Every act of kindness matters, every act of care has a much larger effect than we can see. Every act of cognitive freedom helps break us from the current mold. We are already connected intimately in a network of cause and effect. Everything that we do matters now.

All we have to do is show up and be willing to take responsibility for the world around us. With no guilt for what it is, just a sense of sanity and of care. This is how we begin to stand up internally and heal the world, this is how we begin to become heroes.

CHAPTER FIVE:

RELATIVE REALITY

ཨོ་ཏུ་རེ་ཕྲུ་རེ་ཏུ་རེ་སྱུ་ཏ

The relationship between inner and outer change is direct, and constant. As we change ourselves, the world changes around us. As the world around us changes, we change. This is true both on the levels of our perceptions and our actions. We are, quite literally created by the world and our sensory engagement with it.

Simultaneously our actions, and even our mere presence changes the world around us in both subtle and obvious ways. Even just the act of breathing changes the chemical makeup of the gasses in a room. Every time we are witnessed by someone, their perception of us adds to and interacts with the neural pathways in their brain. Something as simple as the color of our clothing or our body language can affect the people around us in deep ways. We literally change each other every single time we interact, every single time we witness one another in any way.

It is also clear that the way we are currently feeling directly affects our perceptions of the world. If we are tired and hungry, or stressed out, then everything seems to feel a little bit sharper and edgier. We are more likely to react in a short or angry way to people, and things just feel like shit.

Alternatively when we are very happy, or newly in love, everything seems beautiful and gentle. We are more patient and able to handle difficult or stressful situations. When we feel great it seems easier to fully show up in our lives and act from a place of strength.

This may seem obvious and simple, but when we combine it with the idea that we are also constantly being effected and changed by the world around us, it is actually quite profound. There is this ever present trade happening, this direct and relative exchange, between our internal and external worlds. The way we feel changes the way we experience, act and effect world. What

31

happens in the world around us dramatically changes the way we feel.

Our internal and external experiences are seamlessly connected. One constant stream of experience being exchanged between us, the people around us and the reality that we all share. The sense of solid separateness that we have all been trained to feel is mostly an illusion. There are individual brains in individual bodies, but those brains are in no way separate from the world around them. They are quite literally built and created by experience. We are much more like distinct yet connected parts of a continuous landscape than separate beings in any way. There is, for all intents and purposes, no real separation at all.

Underneath the surface, there is a greater dance of cause and effect occurring. Interactions we have with each other at work affect interactions we have when we get home, which in turn affect the other people in our lives. When we are kind to someone in a small way, it can dramatically change their emotional state and the way they interact with everyone else throughout the rest of the day. Our actions act as causes for a myriad of effects that we never see.

Those effects in turn act as causes for endless other effects, speeding out into the great network of human interaction on this earth in an endless and complex chain reaction. This is what is known as global karma. The constant dance of cause and effect that is literally creating and changing us all, every moment of every day. If we were able to zoom out and get a picture of this global interaction, we would be able to see emotional and behavioral trends moving like waves through the sea of human civilization. We would be able to see the pattern of life and it would become clear that we are all entirely interdependent and interconnected.

When we really begin to understand this idea, it becomes clear that working on ourselves on an inner level has great value to the world around us. Not only do we get to experience the positive effects of inner growth and change, our inner growth and evolution as beings also speeds the growth and evolution of society as a whole. The more deeply we work on ourselves, the more we can effect reality in a profound and important way.

Working to develop a kind and flexible mind is one of the most important and brave things we can do for ourselves and the world. If we are able to find in ourselves a place of focused and kind hearted attention, then we can begin to have a very positive effect on the global network of cause and effect. If we are prepared to interact with other people's frustration, anger and negativity from a place of patience and kindness, then we can begin to filter out some of the negativity in the world. We can act as karmic filters. The trick is to allow as many of the negative interactions in your life as possible to pass through you quickly, without allowing them to sit and negatively effect your mindset or your actions.

That is to say, everything that happens to us must be felt, but it doesn't have to sit with us beyond that instant.

Some things affect us in a longer term way no matter what, but we can begin to let go of the smaller instances of stress and negativity in our lives. We don't have to carry a bad interaction in traffic with us beyond the moment that it happens. When someone is rude to us, we can feel how much it pisses us off and then just relax and let it go.

The real surprise here is that the more we allow ourselves to totally feel our initial reaction, the more instantaneously we can let it go. The trick is to learn to feel that anger, frustration or sadness deeply, without acting at all. Just being there and letting it hit us fully, with no tension. We can just be with our breath for a moment and feel exactly whatever we are feeling. You will be surprised at how quickly emotions can move through you and change when you do this.

Every time a negative effect happens in our lives, we have a choice to work with it and do our best to let it go. This is of course much more difficult with trauma and intensely negative interactions, and in this area we should be very gentle with ourselves. However in most cases we have a choice not to pass negativity on into the sea of global cause and effect while also not trying to stuff it away. Furthermore, with a bit of work and attention, we can train ourselves to actually call up love in the face of frustration, fear and anger. All we have to do is remember that we are part of this great network of experience, and whatever we feed into the system both internally and externally, will come back to us in one way or another.

34

Therefore all emotion should be felt, fully and honestly, right there on the spot with as little resistance as possible. Action however, should always be informed by this idea that we are all seamlessly interdependent, and every single thing that we do matters on a global scale.

We are simultaneously at the mercy of this reality and to a large degree, in control of it. What we do with that is up to us.

Through a practice that we will call "Clearing The Heart" we can directly engage with, and release, all of the emotional clutter that gathers throughout a day. Living in this world comes along with a constant barrage of human interaction that we don't always have time or energy to process, particularly on an emotional level. We often feel the need to move past hurtful experience without fully processing and releasing the experience. Over time, we can end up bogged down and worn out in a very deep way. Through the practice of Clearing The Heart we can rejuvenate ourselves deeply while opening our hearts to the truth of daily life.

Here is how it works:

Sit somewhere comfortable and close your eyes. Spend a few moments just feeling your body and noticing your breath. Notice the way your shoulders, chest and stomach rise and fall while you breathe. For a few moments, just be there.

When you feel present in your body and in the moment, gently place your right hand over your heart. If it feels right, you can also place both hands on top of your heart, one over the other. It's important to do this with a very gentle touch, as if you are simply laying your hand on your chest. Take a few breaths with your hand on your heart, just feeling it there. Continue to breathe, feeling the warmth from your hand on your chest and noting the gentle touch of it. Allow that feeling of warmth to grow in your mind, feel the heat of your hand on your heart.

Continue to breathe deeply, doing your best to simply let go into the moment. After a few minutes, you will begin to feel a warm and gentle connection with the heart. When the connection between the heart and your hand feels present and steady, focus on creating the feeling of breathing through the heart. Become aware of any tension or heaviness in the chest as you breathe. As you breathe in, put your mind on your hand and imagine you are pulling out any heaviness, stuckness, sadness or tension that may be in the heart. This feels sort of like your hand is vacuuming out debris from your chest. As you breathe out, allow your heart to feel warm and tender. Then again as you breathe in, use the feeling of your hand collecting and pulling in any uncomfortable or stuck sensations in the chest.

Repeat this process of clearing the chest on the in breath, and allowing the heart to feel warm on the out breath until you feel your hand is "full" or your heart is clear. The idea sounds vague, but trust me at some point the feeling in both your hand and your heart will change. When this happens, take your hand away from your chest and allow it to hang over your chair or cushion. If you like, you can let both hands hang over your chair or touch the ground. The important thing is that you feel the gravity, that your hands and arms feel as if they are relaxed and dangling.

Breathe in through the nose and down into the heart. On the out breath allow all of the heavy and stuck feelings that you have gathered in your hands to "drain out" into the ground. Every breath in goes into the heart, stomach and chest. Every breath out now releases heaviness and stuckness from your hands, down into the ground.

Continue to release the sensation of heaviness or tension into the ground until you feel you are clear and done with the practice. Again, this sounds vague but the sensation will present itself if you listen to your own body and personal experience.

This practice is incredibly powerful and also incredibly subtle. It is one of the best ways we can provide ourselves with emotional and mental self care. This practice of meditating on the heart can help us open up, heal old wounds, and begin to feel more connected to the world around us.

CHAPTER SIX:

IT MIGHT JUST BE A RENAISSANCE

ༀ་མ་ཎི་པ་དྨེ་ཧཱུྂ

The world may be in a very difficult place, but collectively we actually have everything we need to turn this world around. The current and ongoing destruction of our planet is entirely unnecessary, as is the culture of inequality and repression that has arisen in the world throughout our history, and is now becoming so incredibly apparent. These things are simply not the way it needs to be, they can be changed and we have at our fingertips all of the tools we need to create a sustainable, kind, and more equal world.

The only thing that is standing in our way is this feeling of weight and heaviness, this feeling that it is all too much to manage. Powerlessness is something that everyone is feeling, together. Everyone is saying together that they can't fix it alone.

Powerlessness gives us a way out, it can be someone else's problem because "there's nothing I can do about it". But that is simply just not true. If we are willing, collectively, to throw off the chains of fear and dis-empowerment we really can fix this. When I say "this" I literally mean the vast majority of what are considered global or national issues today. The stuff we think we can't fix. Racism, misogyny, environmental destruction, starvation, literally all of it.

Think about it, how many people do you know that have incredible skills and want to see the world in a more compassionate, stable state? How many incredibly talented and powerful people do you know that are saying they just can't change the world as one person. Personally, I know hundreds. I think we all do. There are millions of people out there, sitting in their houses and saying "I just can't do this alone."

There is this incredible fusion of art and culture happening, this new global mind arising with all of the connectivity in the world. How much of a wealth of human brilliance, ingenuity and evolution could be found in a world where there were no impoverished nations?

How much more could we gain as a species if we were to actually care for all of humankind? Imagine how many genius minds we have probably lost throughout history to poverty, racism, misogyny, war etc. How many young brilliant minds have been passed over because they are women in a country where women are afforded no rights? What would have happened if Einstein or Stephen Hawking had been born in the slums of India and never been sent to school, or never been exposed to the scientific community? What would the world have lost without these two brilliant minds?

We are at a time in history that could propel us into a literal golden age. We have all of the necessary resources and technology to end hunger on this earth. We have all of the brilliance and ingenuity that we need to end the global climate crises and move humanity onto sustainable sources of energy. We have access to wisdom, philosophy and social structures that if enacted, could put an end to racism and misogyny in this country and eventually the world. It really is just a matter of priorities.

That is how it is done, that is how human civilization has always improved. Our history is full of people who believed in themselves and forced change. Heroes are simply people who became honest with themselves and decided to follow their inspiration. Heroes are people who believed firmly that they could make a difference, in their own personal way. Heroes are generally just as flawed as any other human being, they are simply willing to focus on their strengths. They are willing to give what they actually have. Ask yourself how you would like to see the world change over the course of your life, because it is the only time you get to change it, and it is a whole lot less time than it seems to be.

All the tools we need are already there. The science, philosophy and abundance of resources that we need are at our fingertips. The truth of kindness is inside of all of us. What we are missing is belief. I will tell you outright, and invite you to read this again and again for it is also a greatly held secret: you are FAR more powerful than you think you are. You have everything that you need to make a difference in this world and contribute to positive change in your own personal way. YOU have what it takes to make the world a better place to live in. Exactly the way you are, right here, right now. We all do. There is nothing wrong with what you are, you are life itself.

If we are willing to take responsibility for the world around us out of a sense of inspiration, then we can make great change. This sense of responsibility only feels heavy when we force it on ourselves, when it is motivated by guilt or fear. But if we can see the parts of the world that we wish were better, both big and small, and feel inspired to bring change then it can feel truly great. When we believe that we can make a very real positive difference in this world, that we can be of benefit to it, then we can act from a place of empowerment and presence. We can allow the feeling of giving to the world to lift us up and give us purpose, to give us a valuable place in the universe.

CHAPTER SEVEN:

THE POWER OF TRUE PRESENCE

ཨོཾ་མ་ཎི་པ་དྨེ་ཧཱུྃ

There is a gentle and profound power that develops from practicing being fully in the moment. There is a gravity to people who are completely here right now. This can seem intangible, but it is a very real skill. We've all met these people, people who seem to have a deep openness about them. A physical presence that gently takes over a room, a person with what the Romans called gravitas. It is a quality that comes from a special combination of self acceptance and total presence of mind. It is one of the great and simple powers available to us.

This type of person has an air of being able to change the world around them, as if they are a defining part of the landscape. These types of people create a feeling of gentle yet deep strength in their presence.. This total hereness of mind is one of the great secrets of true power, and it is entirely trainable, anyone can build this skill. What we are sensing and seeing in these people is unclouded awareness, total presence of sensory and thus visceral experience. They are firmly rooted in feeling the world around them, they are oriented fully to the truth of their experience in the moment and they accept it.

The courage and relaxed precision of being fully here is available to all of us. We just need to be willing to wake up a little bit. We need to find ways to leave the movie in our minds and check in repeatedly, over and over again with what is going on right here right now. With what our bodies are telling us. With what our current actual personal truth is. This is actually the great secret to most meditation and tantric practice: The point is to learn to be totally here, to actively become part of the experience of life with every ounce of our attention and focus, with every cell of our bodies. We have been thoroughly trained

43

to be only partially present, and this allows the current hierarchies of the world to keep us distracted, to keep us seeking instead of finding.

Training true presence can be done in a number of ways, but there are two primary ways that seem to work for us as westerners these days, and humans throughout history. The first one is meditation, which is difficult for some people, but works very well for others. Meditation has certainly proven to be a direct route to full, mindful presence for many people, but we will go into that a bit more later.

The second way is even more direct than meditation for many people these days because it works with our daily experience. The second way is the way of active meditation or tantra and can be done on the spot, in the moment, throughout the day. The idea is to use the senses themselves as a way to train the mind to be present. This is a form of active meditation that has been kept relatively secret throughout history, does not require sitting still and is easy to practice. It is also one of the fastest and most direct routes to "waking up".

The process is simple, has two steps which are ultimately one step, and only requires regularly remembering to do it. It is an ancient tantric practice which has been guarded and veiled, hinted at in many writings and teachings throughout history, but here I will call it zoning in. Here is how it works: whenever possible, we stop the track in our minds and switch directly to feeling the world around us. We can do this with any of the senses, and it is best to practice with each of them. Start by repeatedly noticing how your clothes feel against your skin, how the room or place you are in sounds, how your breath feels in your nose, how the color and form of everything impacts you, how it all smells. There don't have to be any words attached to this experience, in fact it is better if there aren't. The purpose of this practice is to feel your current experience without having to judge or label it mentally. That is to say, the goal here is to have the most purely sensory experience of what is going on as possible, and give over to it repeatedly throughout the day.

The second step, which with practice becomes part of the first step, is to allow these sense perceptions to have an emotional impact on you. In this step lies the real secret. The idea is to come into touch with the visceral feeling of your senses. Not the words attached, but the way your sensory input makes you feel. By training our minds to check in with what's actually going on over and over again, we can come closer to being fully here. More importantly we can begin to see how intimately connected we are to the landscape of sensation around us. We can begin to glimpse the raw truth of human experience. We start to see what is actually going on. After a very short time of doing this, you may be quite surprised with what you find.

Meal times and eating can also be a very powerful way to start a zoning in practice. We often don't take the time to taste our food, fitting it in between busy parts of our day. If you think about it, it's really too bad. Tasting food is one of the great and simple pleasures of life, one of the most obvious and easy routes to pleasant experience. The act of nourishing our bodies can become a time to train the mind and zone in. We can be fully with it.

Try this some time, or even right now. Take a bite of a food that you truly like, and don't skip any part of the experience. Be with it as you bring it to your mouth, be with it as it enters your mouth and let it roll around around on your tongue, feel every single time that you chew. Don't just eat it, really taste it. Feel it as it goes down your throat, feel it as it enters your stomach. Be with it, every single part of the way. Start with one meal per day, decide which one it will be right now if you want to. Dinner is often best for most people, because we usually have more time to relax while eating it.

Using sight can be done most easily at first with bright colors, and then eventually with the form of objects and people. We can begin by picking any deep or bright color, or really any color at all. When you look at it, bring the feeling of seeing to the front of your eyes. Try to see it with the very front parts of your eyes, as if you were focusing on something far off in the distance or something very small. Allow the color to really pop in your mind, allow it to trigger any emotional and physical feelings that come up. Allow the sense of seeing this color to be physically inside of you. This may take a few minutes for some people and be more direct for others. But if you stare at the color for long enough, you will begin to feel something emotional, something in your body. This is the first practice for sight and by training it you will begin to fully experience what it means to see. It's something we have always known, but have been taught to gloss over and ignore.

At any point throughout the day, it is easy to check in with the feeling of our touch and skin. We can notice the feeling of all of our clothes, going from the top of our bodies to the bottom. We can notice the wind on our faces, or the temperature in a room, we can feel our feet on the ground with every step. We can check in with input from parts of our bodies we usually ignore, we can feel our toes or our calves or the bottoms of our feet with every step. The trick here is to again be fully with it for at least a few moments, as many times as possible throughout the day. Just actually allow yourself to fully and completely feel touch with no distraction or internal description.

This kind of practice is a whole lot like weight training or cardio for our minds. It trains our awareness in the present moment to a laser like precision over time, giving us access to our full power in live stream. It sharpens our senses. With practice, we begin to naturally zone in more and more throughout the day, until we reach a full synchronization of sensory experience. Life becomes a constantly evolving true and clean glimpse of our own personal depth as humans. A way of being which is at least partially always anchored to the truth of the present moment. Our personal truth, the truth without words.

47

The truth that we feel. This is one of the fastest ways to build gravitas, to live life completely with every centimeter of your body, with every sensation moment by moment. To actually be here.

It is also the first step to sensing the world around you on a greater level, it is the first step to noticing what is going on around you in a whole new way. Believe me that at some point in this practice, the world will just open up. Or rather you will just open up, and all at once you will find this great power that has been waiting for you to claim it. You will begin to notice things about the world and yourself that you had never noticed before. But the trick is to not fight your mind and distractions, just notice them. Continue to appreciate the process of planning, but feel your feet on the ground and the pen in your hand as you write the plan. Feel your determination for a better future right now.

In a very direct and truthful way, we are our senses, and in this lies a well hidden secret. The secret of actual reality without confusing concepts attached. The secret of the way it all actually just looks, feels, sounds and tastes in a naked and honest way. Not the way you are supposed to experience things, but instead the way you actually experience them. Eventually this can lead us to direct experience, what zen calls satori. Experience with no conceptual hindrance. A way of being that frees the mind to be spontaneous and inspired by the present moment. This is one of the fastest and most direct ways to wake up, and it is has been guarded like a secret jewel by mystical cultures throughout history. If you practice with your senses this way, your experience of the world will change. You will begin to see and experience things in a different way.

You may begin to feel the raw truth.

CHAPTER EIGHT:

CHASING THE CARROT

ཨོཾ་མ་ཎི་པདྨེ་ཧཱུྃ

We live in a world that is constantly running forward, that is always looking to the future and the next moment, or always reminiscing about the past. Everything is about planning and where we will be later, or where we have been. We spend our work days thinking about our nights, and by the time we get to our nights all we can seem to do is talk and think about our work days. By pointing this out I do not mean to say that planning itself is somehow bad or negative, only that we have been trained to be so obsessed with what is not yet or what used to be, that we have forgotten how to be with what is right now. This has become a neurosis for our society, in which we never want to truly look at the tools at hand, we just want to build.

We of course want to move forward in our lives with a

plan, there is no arguing that. But the absolute truth is, all we ever get is now. One continuous now. Living primarily in a state of planning ahead actually makes the act of planning itself almost useless.

This is because if all we know how to do is plan, to leave the current situation in our minds then no amount of planning really matters. By the time our plans come to fruition, we are not there to experience them. We are already onto the next idea of the future, never fully enjoying or experiencing what we have worked so hard to create. You may say "of course I enjoy my life.", and I am sure you do! But if you really think about it, you may notice how rarely we are fully here, present in the moment. How often the mind just flies away in some random direction, sometimes happy sometimes painful.

The absolute fact is that it is now, always has been now and always will be now. We never actually get to live in the past or the future, for they are both creations of our memory and imagination.

Although this may seem like a subtle concept, it is one of the primary mechanisms by which our power has been stolen from us. Through a very detailed societal construct, we have been taught to ignore the current moment in a deeply profound and fundamental way. A way that we are not even fully aware of. If we don't stop and notice how distracted we are, it never even dawns on us that this lack of presence is occurring. And that is exactly how they want it. The idea is to keep you looking forward, keep you chasing some possible future, instead of stopping and

51

seeing what is actually going on right now. We have been taught to check out of the current moment and plan forward in every possible way. Our society is to a large extent built upon this idea of blindly rushing forward, running from some dark past, without ever embracing what we currently are.

I will again preface the rest of this chapter by saying that planning itself, preparing for the future by way of schooling and participating in society is fundamentally good. It makes sense; it is how we grow. There is no attempt here to debunk that. However this plan for the future is only a concept, never actually real, always one day away. It is useful to have a map and a plan, but life is lived by taking short glimpses of the map and then being with the path itself. We don't hike a trail in the forest with the map right in front of our faces, if we did we would trip as we walked and miss the beauty of the hike. So in a way this is a challenge. Can you accept the fact that planning can be useful, while still remaining committed to living in the present moment?

From the very start of life in this society, we are taught to chase the carrot hanging on a string. School is at first about being present with childhood, for about the first year in kindergarten. But from there on out, we are taught to think about the next test, the next grade, our future jobs and our future selves. We are asked from a very young age "What do you want to be when you grow up?" Asked to define ourselves before we know the world and subtly being taught that focusing on what is here right now has less value than thinking ahead and planning for the future.

This continues into high school, with the focus of the entire experience being the preparation for adulthood. We are constantly pressured for our test scores, our abilities at sports, our social abilities, our "extracurricular skills". We are taught to obsess over our potential for tomorrow, but tomorrow never really comes. When it does, when we do ace that test or win that basketball game it is seen as only a stepping stone towards our future. It is a check mark on our growing resume, the piece of paper that somehow proves our worth. At some point, if we are lucky, someone in our lives tells us to slow down and feel our feet on the ground. To check in with the experience of being here now. But these people are few and far between, and largely our childhood is literally stolen from us. Sacrificed by our parents and mentors on the pyre of some conceptual future that never really seems to arrive.

And so we progress, into adulthood.

At this point we have probably accomplished quite a bit, but are still waiting for the moment when we get to stop and taste it. We hit 18 or 21, we feel free and empowered to be "adults" now. But what we find is that nothing really changes. If anything the safety net falls out and we find ourselves free falling towards some distant and non existent future. College begins, we are told we have to choose a major, we still only focus on what we can become instead of what we actually are. We seek a mate with the idea of finding a wife or husband, someone we can spend our lives with. The focus is still always on the future and we keep chasing the carrot. We become trained to see every situation and every person as simply a stepping stone towards some undefined future in which we finally get to stop and be happy. This creates a kind of base level agitation, an annoyance or anxiety that arises from our desire to push time forward and really get somewhere.... but we are so rarely actually just in the act of being anywhere at all.

College ends, we find a job and probably a mate. We get married and finally we think, life starts. But now the focus is on career growth and retirement. We focus on whether or not our marriage will "make it." We focus on if our kids will "make it" as adults and we miss out on them being kids. We take so many pictures that we forget what it's like just to see something profound happen without having to document it. We spend so much time wondering if the future will work out in some dreamlike and perfect way, while desperately comparing it to the past. The problem is, that at some level we know the truth. In some deeper, more fundamentally aware part of ourselves we know that this path of always wondering how it will "end" actually does lead to the end. It strikes us all at once sometime in our 30's or 40's that the end is actually our deaths, and if we elaborate on this idea to it's conclusion, that is all we are actually chasing. Our own end. "Will it all work out in the end?"... At some point we begin to realize that rushing towards that end is not necessarily what we want to do.

Eventually we get that golden ticket, our retirement. We are told that now we finally get to stop and enjoy life, that we can live on the money we have saved and spend time with our adult children and grandchildren. This is fantastic and we are finally told by society that it is OK to stop, to have a genuine and honest human experience in the moment. A human experience that is based upon what is right here right now and simply being with it all at once. But why could we not have had that for our entire lives? Why couldn't each and every single moment be drank in fully, lived deeply and honestly exactly the way it is?

Throughout our lives we have glimpses of this totally present mind. It shows up on vacation, or when we are on the dance floor or when we are making love. We touch it briefly when we go to a museum or a beautiful park. We notice that full and present moment in a bite of our favorite food or in a sunset. We see it in our friend's and family's eyes. It hits us as we fall in love, or smell a perfect spring flower. Throughout our lives we get to touch the feeling of actually being here, actually being fully alive and present for a moment and it is wonderful. So wonderful in fact that we even begin to chase that presence, but there is still a fundamental confusion because we seek it outside of ourselves. We forget the deep and intrinsic value of our present experience.

The truth is though, that this present and joyful, celebratory presence of life is constantly available and it is one of the true sources of human power. All we have to do is begin to notice how distracted and anxious we are about the future and the past. All we have to do is practice just being here in every possible way, letting it in and even enjoying it for what it is right now. The antidote is in the poison.

Here I would like to present to you a very straight forward practice, called "Finger Counting" that we can use to train our ability to anchor the mind in the present moment. It combines breath meditation with mudra practice, an ancient tantric yoga practice which involves holding the hands in particular positions while meditating. In this practice, we have simplified the presentation of mudra by removing any religious connotations, while preserving the meditative and cognitive benefit.

This practice can be done standing up, sitting down, lying down or just about in any position where you can

56

move your hands. You can do this with your eyes open or closed, although it is often more powerful done with the eyes shut.

Take a normal breath in, and exhale a normal breath out. When your lungs are empty, before the next inhalation, touch the tips of your thumb and pointer finger. Then breathe in and out again normally. When your lungs are empty, before you inhale again, move your thumb to touch your middle finger. Then breathe in and out again normally, allowing yourself to focus on the feeling of the breath in your nose and throat. This time in between breaths move your thumb to touch your ring finger. Again, breathe in and out normally, then in between breaths move the thumb to touch the tip of the pinky finger. For the fifth breath, open the hands so that the palms show, as if you were waving. Continue by starting again with the thumb touching the pointer finger and move through each finger, one breath at a time.

You can do this practice with one hand at a time, but it is best done with both hands simultaneously. It is good to set a number of "full hands" to count through, for example I often choose to do four hands worth at a time. This means that I count a breath for each finger, and a fifth one for an open hand, four times in a row. You can however, also choose to simply sit and do this for a particular amount of time, or just for as long as you would like with no need to measure the time or repetitions. Finger Counting meditation can provide a fantastic time to just rest our minds in the moment. There doesn't need to be a whole lot of trying or strenuous effort involved. We can just be with the breath and the feeling of our hands.

Finger counting is a powerful way to anchor the mind into the present, physical and visceral experience. Try doing four or five hands worth a day for two weeks and you will begin to notice a gentle sharpening of your mind. Through practicing this way on a regular basis, the present moment will become more accessible and it will become more natural to be here, in the now.

CHAPTER NINE:

FLIPPING THE COIN OF THE INNER MONOLOGUE

ༀ་མ་ཆི་པ་དྲེ་ཧཱུྃ

We all have an inner voice, an inner monologue running on a constant loop. It consists of things we are afraid of, things we are excited about, things we love and things we hate. It consists of our hopes, and our fears that those hopes will not come true. It speaks in the tongue of judgment, deciding and parsing everything that we see, hear, and do. We listen to it all day, sometimes much to our dislike and annoyance. It plays in the back of our heads, sometimes quieting but always returning.

If we listen to the contents of it, if we honestly pay attention, we will probably find that this voice can be quite nasty. Our inner monologue speaks to us, we speak to ourselves, in ways we would never dream of speaking to another human being. It tells us when we fail, it tells us when we feel stupid or ashamed, often in dark and aggressive ways. It's almost as if we have an inner bully that most of us are carrying around, ready to jump down our throats the moment we make the smallest mistake. This is actually entirely normal for modern people. It is a widespread internal phenomena that has arisen as a side effect of our culture, and it is one of the mechanisms by which we are robbed of our power. It is the most consistent chain holding us from freedom, the great internal and secretly held pain of our society. This voice has been trained into us, implanted into our consciousness by a society that worships the concept of lack.

You can see it when you make a mistake and that heavy handed part of your inner workings say "that was SO stupid". When that feeling in your chest or shoulders tells you that you messed up and you should feel terrible about it. When you forget your keys, or are late or say the wrong thing in a social setting. The internal beat up mechanism arises. It's always there, waiting to tell us what we did wrong. We can hear it in our heads and feel it in our bodies.

The idea of wanting to self improve, to know when we have made mistakes and self correct is obviously a fantastic human quality. One we need desperately. It is so important to be aware of how we want to grow and change, and to put our minds on a goal. This is of course a wonderful thing. The problem comes from relating to this human quality of self correction in a fundamentally negative, aggressive and masochistic way. It often goes beyond being helpful and becomes simply self abusive. It holds us down and it is a trained mechanism that has been taught to us since childhood.

What is important to understand is that this tendency to be fundamentally negative with ourselves is not only painful, it is dysfunctional. It serves us to a point, we can push ourselves aggressively for a while, but eventually it breaks down. We aren't really able to operate in the world like this long term. At least not without feeling totally exhausted and developing a mistrust in ourselves.

For many of us, this internal shame mechanism can easily grow throughout our lives. Reinforced again and again via media and confusing social standards. Eventually when this tendency gets out of hand, we can end up just feeling naturally ashamed to be here, to exist at all. This sense can be very subtle, it is easy to not even be fully aware of it. We feel like we always have to be doing something or presenting something in an effort to justify our existence. We don't know what to do with our hands so we pick up our phones. We don't know what to do in a social setting so we awkwardly make small talk.

61

We don't feel comfortable being ourselves here and now, so we run away internally. We judge ourselves for just doing nothing, for existing the way we are.

Being around others, particularly people we don't know, can become an incredible burden. We wonder if they can see the same negative qualities that we see. We wonder if they can see how fat we are, or if we are balding. We wonder if they can see our wrinkles. We wonder if they can see how late we were for work this morning, or how scattered we really feel inside. We wonder if they can see our traumas. We wonder if the people we interact with can see all of the negative qualities that we see in ourselves.

If we aren't careful, we can end up basing large portions of our social interactions on a fear that people can see through us, that they are staring at the exact part of us that we dislike so much. Again, the problem is not the desire to change and grow, the problem is the fixation on the parts of ourselves that we view as not working or wrong. The problem is feeling this constant anxious need to prove ourselves in any way at all.

It is easy to want to say that this is not going on inside of you, it is easy to feel defensive as you read this. I get that. I've been there. When this idea was first presented to me, I didn't feel comfortable accepting it as true. But I have a feeling that if you really look inside yourself, as I have, you will find this internal shame. This deep fear of being what you actually are. This is not at all your fault, it has been implanted in you by the moral, spiritual, and societal constructs that we live under

The negative aspect of this quality in us is not a natural part of being human. We aren't programmed before birth to view ourselves in a fundamentally negative way. So why do we? Where does this mental habit come from? It is a combination of factors in our societal paradigm. In many ways we are consistently trained not to fail instead of being trained to succeed.

These two things may sound synonymous, and in some way they are. They are however two different sides of the same coin. We are trained to look at the world based upon what we don't have. We are taught to look at our lives as fundamentally lacking in some way and requiring change. We can see all the things that others have that we want.

We often base our world view on acquiring all of the traits and things that people have that we somehow don't. We can see perfect abs in a magazine, we can see the car that we wish we had, we can see the perfect relationship that other people have and think "Why don't I have that? How can I get it too?". We can see all the possibility in the world and allow it to make us feel like a failure. When we focus on not failing we tend to note lightly when we succeed, but focus strongly on feelings of loss and shame. We can often end up missing the best parts of ourselves. This is a poverty mindset, one that focuses on lack, and it keeps us very firmly under control.

In this way we are driven with negative reinforcement and fear of pain. It causes us to primarily pay attention to what we don't have. To pay attention to lack. It causes us to develop a feeling of internal poverty, a hole that always desperately needs to be filled. This is exactly how they want it. If you believe you always need something more to justify and prove your worth, then you will easily agree to keep running in the rat wheel that has been set up for us.

This fundamentally negative view seems to be based on the idea that it is somehow bad to be human. There seems to be some deep social shame to just being absolutely whatever we are, not necessarily doing anything, just being here in the moment. We are on some level made anxious by the idea of not constantly having a task or some defined purpose. We seem to collectively feel that there is always some deep dysfunction to fix in the basis of being human. We seem to think that the only way to strive forward is to refuse to admit what is really going on inside of us. The concept of original sin is possibly the most glaringly obvious example, however we are inundated with this shame programming from many directions.

The most ironic part of this situation is that we are typically most ashamed of what we all share. We all get old, we all die and grow wrinkles, we all eat food and could become overweight or fat or too skinny easily, most of us have sexual urges, most of us are to some degree concerned about money, most of us have family difficulties, most of us will experience great anger, sorrow, and anxiety many times throughout life, we all fart.

Even addiction is a natural human pitfall possible for all to experience. Yet we judge the alcoholics in our lives. Even though we know we could also become an addict given the right collection of difficult life experiences. But it is on the basis of our most fundamental human qualities that we are so often ashamed. We beat ourselves up, and often judge others, for simply being human at all. We are even ashamed of our shame, a shame that so many of us seem to share.

What I am proposing is that there is a very simple, yet incredibly dynamic shift we could make in the way we view what it means to be human. A shift that would not only be a far more enjoyable way to live, but would also be a far more functional and productive way to meet our goals of growth and change.

If we flip this view to focusing on how and when we succeed while being lightly aware of doing our best not to fail, then we can be primarily driven by inspiration while still being aware of what can get in our way and how we need to improve. The trick is to learn to focus on opportunity instead of necessity.

In this way of viewing things, we focus on our strengths and learn to use them to the best of our abilities. We remain aware and honest about ways we could grow and improve, but we we don't feel the need to force ourselves to be something we are not. We don't feel the need to fixate on every single mistake. The mistakes are noted as learning experiences, but beyond that lesson, the experience of failure is quickly dropped from our focus. We just sweep it out the door. We know we will fail, we expect it, we welcome it as a learning experience. But our eyes are always on the parts of ourselves that are naturally present and strong. We fixate purposefully, on the ways in which we grow and learn, and the success that comes from that. We stop listening to the nonsense programming that we aren't good enough, are fundamentally broken and have to constantly fight failure. We reclaim our power, and make no room for any person, belief structure or mental habit that holds us down. We simply don't have time for it.

This sounds like the axiom about "glass half full, glass half empty". It sounds like simple optimism vs pessimism. But it is a bit more than that, and I will tell you directly that it is one of the deciding factors of true happiness and fulfillment. Being driven by inspiration sets us free.

It takes some time, but the more we practice this way of thinking, seeing the possibility of success in the world instead of the possibility of failure, seeing opportunity instead of necessity, the more creative we become. The more driven we become, because we can actually see the sun on the horizon. We learn to trust that the world actually does contain what we need, and we can get it. This is one of the great secrets of genius, seeing the possibility of success in the world and focusing on it. There is a great freedom in that.

A deep part of the reason that we are so internally aggressive stems from the fact that we have a backwards sense of what the word "ego" means. On this topic we have been taught fundamentally confusing lie. We seem to conflate self-confidence and belief in our personal abilities with some sort of "unhealthy" or selfish ego. This can be true sometimes, but only if we show up as if we have something to prove. Only if we are pushy about it. Only if we seek to hold others down by being proud and appreciative of ourselves. Saying that it is always negative to be "full of oneself'" is in fact a very oppressive and fundamentally hypocritical view. It leaves little room for us to be proud of ourselves, and thus focus on our personal good qualities.

Being proud of yourself and your potential, even broadcasting that confidence in a comfortable and assured way, is not "negative ego". We should be loud and proud of what we are. It is in fact incredibly brave to be in love with your strengths, so long as it comes with the idea that every single person can also be great. So long as your pride does not seek to hold anyone else down, and makes room for everyone to realize their own greatness, then it is a noble quality of bravery. We can use it to inspire people around us and to be incredibly productive on our own personal paths through life. We should wholeheartedly accept the power and responsibility of beings queens and kings of our own worlds.

So where do we start? We start by noticing the times when we are internally shaming ourselves. We simply engage in the act of noticing our inner monologue when it pops up and noting when we are using shame and fear to motivate ourselves. Hear the voice in your head, or feel the shame in your body and simply become aware of it, simply see it for what it is: a noble attempt to grow using a painful and dysfunctional set of tools that we have been

67

taught to use by fundamentally confused people. We don't have to be angry at ourselves for having this internal monologue, we can just notice it and be with it for a moment. Being aware of what it actually is. That awareness alone will begin to cause the negative internal habits to melt.

After a few days of this, or maybe a week, this tendency to notice our internal monologue will become somewhat automatic. At this point, we can begin to change the course of the way we speak to ourselves towards a tone of inspiration and joy. At this point we must be careful not to shame ourselves for the shame. We can simply be happy to be going through the process of letting it go. This can be a bit of a process, but if we do it in a surgical and precise way then we truly can get somewhere. You can remove this programming, and you will be free in a way that many people are not when you do. Trust me, it's worth it.

We first need to start by deciding that we want to regard ourselves as a friend. That we want to regard ourselves as a workable human being, worthwhile of love and joy. The trick is to see the choice between shame or inspiration, necessity or opportunity, as two sides of the same coin. The coin represents our desire to grow and improve. You can then be very precise in seeing the negative aspect of the desire to grow, and flip the coin over to inspiration.

The way to do this is simple: concentrate on the goal or desired outcome and find the way in which it inspires you. Identify with the feeling of having completed a task, the

feeling of success. Look for the gentlest and most
inspirational way you could phrase it to yourself, as if you
were talking to a dear friend that needed to be cheered up.
Regard yourself as a friend and then try to re-write the
inner script to fit the way you would speak to a friend.
This may sound very corny, but it is in fact incredibly
brave. In this we get to the real core of the problem, the
real deep seeded issue that causes most interpersonal and
even global issues: the lack of synchronization between
the inner and outer experience.

CHAPTER TEN:

SYNCHRONIZING THE INNER AND OUTER EXPERIENCE

ༀ་མ་ཎི་པདྨེ་ཧཱུྂ

In taking an honest look at what it means to be so internally judgmental while trying to be kind and open to the people around us, we can see that we are in what is a comically absurd situation. On the one hand, we are trying to be patient, polite and understanding with others. Most of us are actually doing our best to be as loving and helpful to the people in our lives as we can, it's natural and it feels good. We know on some deeper level, that being as kind as possible is the right thing to do as humans on this earth.

However, as I am also sure you know from life experiences, our inner world and the way we are feeling has a dramatic effect on the way we show up and behave in the world. If we are grumpy from lack of sleep, or sad because of a major life event, or stressed out about this or that, then it becomes more difficult to be friendly and kind. It becomes more difficult to show up in a happy way. This is obvious from our daily lives.

When we take a step back and look at our natural desire to be kind and loving with the people in our lives, combined with our tendency to be cruel to ourselves inside, we can see that it is a broken machine. It is incredibly difficult to be kind to others when your base level habit of internal workings is even a little bit masochistic and cruel. Our outer behavior and experience is a direct mirror of our internal workings.

We are trying to work with a fundamental desynchronization of our inner and outer experience. The way treat others is out of sync with the way we treat ourselves. Living this way is actually quite painful. It can and does lead to great depression for some people. This is why so many people have that creepy aura of "fake nice". It's like they are trying to smile while someone is stabbing them to death. It has a fake and almost disturbing feeling, it stinks of being inauthentic. On the inside there is great aggression towards self, so what we are actually seeing is

71

aggression covered with an intellectually based smile. It is not actually emotionally derived, it is based on the pure conceptual thought that this person wants to be nice. So it feels fake.

This is also why it can be so easy for some people to fly off the handle and say things they don't mean. They are mirroring their inner monologue on the outside. Over time, faking in this way can be incredibly depressing as the distance between the way we want to act towards others and the way we act towards ourselves grows. It creates a precipice for us to fall into. We wonder more and more on a deep level how we could possibly "fit" into the world. Our inner workings are telling us to be kind to others while being rough with ourselves.

The natural conclusion of this thought process is that we really can't be worth very much at all. You may have an ability to be self motivated and defeat this tendency most of the time, but the battle is still always there. Our inherent value as human beings, our right to simply exist and not be totally perfect is questioned more and more as the relationship between outer and inner becomes more and more out of synch. The powers that be feed off of this inner shame cycle and use it to motivate us as they see fit, to buy whatever, shop wherever, say whatever or act however. All because they have you convinced that you aren't worthy just as you are.

This is where the true shame comes in. We tell ourselves that everyone else is deserving of love, but we are deserving of a heavy hand. This comparison often becomes constant, creating a situation where we are always looking to see if others are judging us or seeing us as badly we see ourselves. Eventually many people either give in and become incredibly heavy handed and cruel, incredibly defensive and anxious, live some half hearted presentation of love and care, or grow incredibly depressed. Often it is some terrible combination of all of the above.

Thankfully there is a simple answer. There is a simple way out. But it requires true bravery, the type of bravery that it takes to be corny and not shy away. *To feel vulnerable and open, and maybe even a bit uncomfortable but to sit with it, to bravely not turn away.*

The solution is deep, indestructible, and unquestioning inner kindness. The solution is to turn our love inside and allow it to radiate out from within us. This is in fact the most responsible and strongest thing we can do. In this way we become a benefit to the world instead of a burden. We begin to truly believe that we can find that inner strength we need. We also know that we are deserving of love, success and joy. We know that we are actually just fine the way we are, the same way we would say it to someone we love. We know that it is literally our unarguable birth right to exist on this planet, right here, right now. So we stop feeling so ashamed.

We start with acceptance, because you truly can't change anything at all until you are willing to sit down and take good long look at it. Until you are willing to accept it for what it is, exactly the way it is. Acceptance is key, otherwise it is a bit of a crazy situation. Trying to change something without accepting it is like trying build a house with your eyes closed. Hammering nails without looking at what you are doing. If you don't look clearly at the situation and let it be what it is, then you can't actually work with it and make any real change. So we start by accepting these inner tendencies of negative self view. We start by seeking them out. We do our best to see them for what they are. We do our best to see where they originate from in our personal stories. In seeing the parts of ourselves that we fear the most, and bringing them love, we can begin to bring them into reign.

In this way we can start to see how to flip the coin of inner speech to one of love, acceptance and inspiration. This will be a little bit different for everyone, but the focus should always be on acceptance and inspiration. If we don't feel inspiration we can start by simply being ok to be here. Just here, as we are, right now.

If we can do this, we start to see an automatic and wonderful change in the way we relate to the world around us. We begin to become spontaneously kind and actually truly take joy at our success and the success of others. You can see it in someone's eyes when they truly have developed love and acceptance for themselves. There is a gentleness to them, a loving quality that is at once sharp and soft. It cuts through us. We have all had that friend, family member or acquaintance that there is love and joy just rolling off of. That person who always makes you feel a bit more comfortable with yourself. This is because they feel comfortable with themselves on an internal level, so they are easily able to give that same kindness away on a social level. This can easily be a trained skill, it just takes some time. But in the end, it truly is one of the major keys to lasting fulfillment and happiness. In the ability to appreciate exactly what we are fully, we find our true power as human beings.

CHAPTER ELEVEN:

BEING SEEN AND HOLDING SPACE

There is a part of us that feels a need to be known, a need to be seen. The validation of another human being giving our experience their full attention is valuable beyond measure. This quality of really being with someone's deep inner truth no matter how messy, is what defines friendships. People we can talk to that will really listen can be hard to find. This is very sad, because we all share this need to be genuinely seen and heard.

These days, we are glimpsed quickly over and over again, but not really seen very often at all. This can be a great cause of sadness and depression. We are surrounded by people, on the train, on the bus, in traffic, on an elevator, on the street and none of them are seeing us. We are often packed into situation where vast quantites of people are trying not to see us. On a subconscious level this can be quite damaging.

Throughout our history as human beings we have been social. Our ability to band together and create a commonly good outcome is a large part of what defines us as a species. This dates back all the way to our discovery and mastery of fire. The ancient discovery of starting fire did not just act as a great tool, it created a coming together. With this discovery human kind didn't just get a fire to cook on, we got a fire to gather around. Here we find a very important part of the truth.

Throughout our evolution, we have rarely been in contexts where we would come together yet be totally ignored the way we find ourselves on an elevator or train. For the vast majority of human history if you were in the same place as someone, they either knew you and cared for you or were trying to kill you. City culture has only truly existed as it does now for a fraction of our time as a species. This tendency to need to be seen is obvious in the behavior of a child that is ignored.

If you leave a child in a room full of people and no one even looks at them, they will quickly fall back on attention seeking behavior. At first they will try to get attention in a

77

good way, tugging on people's clothes and touching them, but after a while the child will begin to act out. They will do whatever it takes to gain attention, tantrum, scream, roll around on the floor, anything. The child will become more and more desperate until someone pays attention. This same feeling is at work deeply inside of all of us.

Over time, being passed by again and again without any acknowledgment can start to create a closing in, a subtle fearfulness and shame. This can be almost imperceptible, and people deal with it in different ways. Nonetheless we are faced with the challenge of feeling seen in a swirling world full of people and distractions. It can be quite difficult.

What I am trying to say here is that if we want to evolve collectively, if we want to band together and move forward, then we need to be willing to really see each other. We need to be willing to make eye contact with strangers and linger in it for a second, of course using our discretion to keep ourselves safe. There are some situations where it makes sense to keep to ourselves, but they are more rare than we probably think. In treating everyone as valuable we are able to commit a great act of radical social change.

But more than strangers, we need to be willing to really see and hear our friends. We need to be willing to be with them and simply witness what they are, hold space for them to fill in with their own truth. This is one of the most valuable gifts we can give to someone, a gift that is becoming harder and harder to find. In the midst of all of this change and influx of information, we must be willing to stop and simply be with each other clearly and with no distractions.

Sit with the people you care about and really try to feel their experience, see all of them, not just what they want you to see. Drink in the experience and show yourself to them. In general, most people don't so much need help, they just need to be seen. To be loved exactly as they are and to be empowered. We all need this, so it would make sense to focus on giving it to one another.

Evolving and growing past the destructive and terrible parts of the world is possible if we are willing to do it together. If we are willing to see and honor each other exactly the way we are.

CHAPTER TWELVE:

DIRECT EXPERIENCE: BREAKING THE CHAINS OF CONCEPTUAL ILLUSION

ཨོཾ་ཨཱཿ཈ིཔ་ཌྲེ་ཧཱུྃ

There is a layer of thought on top of our experience of reality which creates a necessary and useful illusion. It is the names and labels we have learned to apply to things and experiences around us. It is the explanation that we have been taught to give it all. The way we have learned to parse, dissect, and define each part of our experience of being human as separate. That is a chair, that is blue, that is green, that is a car, this is anger, this is happiness, this is spicy, that is bland etc. It is our conceptual interpretation of the world, and it is very very useful.

By dividing our experience of the world up into concepts, we are able to communicate with each other. We are able to build plans, we are able to imagine things that don't exist and then create them. We are able to create language and art, to express ourselves. Thanks to conceptual expression, we are able to create civilization itself. This is the stroke of brilliance of being human, the ability to imagine and then create. The ability to conceptualize the world around us and then envision change. The problem is only that the way we experience and use this incredible skill is backwards to the way it actually functions. We are misunderstanding the cause and effect of experience and concept, which can be a source of great confusion and pain.

The powers and hierarchies that currently exist have applied a very careful layer of control to our perceptions. This is done in a precise and methodical way with a subtle yet powerful hate for what it is to be human. They have taught us to see the world as a series of concepts and symbols that they control. In school, in church, on TV or in our families we are taught what is "right" and what is "wrong". We are taught to listen and regurgitate, never being told to follow our own inner compass and define things for ourselves. We are taught the "right way" to dance, to speak, to think, to write, to express and to feel. Even our deepest emotions are repressed, with anger, anxiety and sadness being demonized as off putting and wrong or labeled as "bad/negative emotions".

81

From the moment we enter the societal construct of school as children we are taught what the powers that be feel is the "right" way to be human. We learn it through the symbols and concepts that are presented to us. These concepts define the way we actually think and perceive the world around us. This poison runs very deeply in our veins, because it defines the way in which we view the entire world and ourselves. It is the overarching method by which we are controlled and held down as a massive herd of sheep.

The secret to realize here is that the concepts themselves, as powerful as they are, are not the source of experience in your mind. They are not the deepest or even most true form of experience. They are secondary to experience; a means to elaborate. Concepts, at their root, are in the imagination, a useful illusion that we all agree upon (to some degree). So when we deal only in a world of concepts and labels, a world of useful imaginations, then we can become incredibly disoriented and confused. Everything ends up being seen and experienced only in comparison to the imagination and illusion that we have attached to it. Eventually we can end up relating to life as a pile of concepts, all intertwined with one another, forgetting the raw experience involved. The raw experience that the concepts are originally based upon.

So, for example when you go outside on a cold winter's day, you have this full and raw experience that is complete in every way. Your face numbs, your heart races, you wake up a bit, the hair on your arms stands up, you

82

take in the snow and the scene visually, hear the wind in the trees.... this whole entire raw sensory experience happens. When you go back inside and describe what happened to someone else you say "It's cold and windy, there is snow." This is useful in getting across the idea, but it is a secondary and in fact very poor label for the experience of being there on the porch in the cold. It doesn't quite get across the truth of it. The person you are describing it to is left to imagine it themselves using the concepts you have presented.

This is fine, and again quite useful. All sorts of incredible art comes from this attempt to fully express the human experience and condition using concepts. But when we lose ourselves entirely in conceptual reality, without checking in regularly with the absolute truth of just being here, then we live in a world of illusions. More so, we live in a world of assumptions, trying to describe the world to ourselves through the language we have been taught.

This is partially what is described as "relative reality" and "absolute reality" in eastern explanations of the world. This is what they mean by being "empty". They don't actually mean emptiness, they mean being so free of concepts that you are a constant vessel for the experience of the present moment. Vast openness is probably a better translation than "empty". They mean becoming one with the sensory input and emotional response that is available right here, right now. Free of words and complicated interpretations. The feeling.

83

The brilliance of teaching us to forget raw reality and rely on concepts, is that now we can be very easily controlled. When the world is simply a complex building of concepts, then the concepts themselves begin to limit and define your reality. We can be told that we are the concept of "bad" because we have not fulfilled the concept of "good", we can be told that there is a "right way" to experience life. We can be constrained and directed, culled and controlled. I will say right now very clearly that if there is any mechanism by which you are being held down and controlled by a hierarchy it is this idea of conceptual reality. The vast majority of religions and governments have been used as a tool of repression in this way at some point in history. This is the greater issue at work, and it is at first very difficult to grasp.

By convincing us as children that everything was a symbol for something else, that there was nothing beyond the expression of experience, no inherent value to just standing somewhere and being with the experience of it on the spot, they cut us off from our own power of free thought. By insisting that things are what we are told they are, the powers that be are able to define reality as they see fit. They are able to feed us the "truth" as they see it, and we have been trained to eat it right up. They are able to make us all fit into the perfect little pigeon holes that they want us in, consuming and obsessing over "the end", never taking much time to just wake up and make our own decisions about the experience that we are having.

What I am saying is shocking and actually quite easy to

ignore, for the mental construct that has been designed for us to live our lives out in is quite an ingeniously designed cage. A cage that has been designed to be invisible, yet hold you none the less. I will tell you outright that this has been done to you on purpose, but the actual people involved were also slaves to the social construct. I truly hope that you are listening right now, that you are totally taking this in. Here it is, right in front of you: By telling you that you must define the world at every possible moment, that you must parse your experience down into concepts that then have to fit nicely together in a perfect construct, they have convinced you to sign up for a form of mental and emotional slavery that holds most of us down for our entire lives. They have stolen your independence as a mind and individual before you were even fully aware that you had it, and they didn't even know they were doing it. It wasn't taught to you maliciously, they simply taught you what they know.

There is a very direct and easy way that you can see this truth right now. Try to look at the words on this page, or any letter or number and experience it without it's symbolic meaning. That is to say, pick a letter or word on this page and try to see it as a set of lines and shapes instead of a symbol that has some extra meaning attached. Try to see it as you would art, or a photograph. Allow the letter to be what it is as a visual experience without your mind having to explain it at all. Feel the first thought, the one before cognitive understanding. It may take a moment, but if you stare and just let yourself see, it will happen. You will glimpse the absolute reality of the word or letter in front of you. The absolute reality of a spoken word can be heard and felt when we repeat the word over and over again. Eventually, the word becomes meaningless, and our experience is the sound. The true sound. There is great power in this, power you probably don't even realize. In fact, according to many mystical traditions, I just told you something that I am really not supposed to tell you at all. I hope you were paying attention.

Direct experience can be felt more and more as we zone in and simply feel the world around us in a raw and open state. With no judgments at all. In this way we become more and more oriented to the truth of life, to the reality of what is going on around us, free of the crazy little dramas in our heads, the programs that have been put there. It;s not necessarily that the nonsense in our head totally goes away, just that we begin to see through it, we begin to laugh at it.

In this way we begin to actually become part of the landscape around us, and we find it is much more easy to mold the flow of life to our choosing. When this happens we have begun to meet our inner master, the part of ourselves that we know is aware, that is always here, anchored and unchanging, yet made of change itself. Our raw and personal awareness that is found through the simple act of being present in our current experience fully.

The trick is to regularly return to the rawness of your

experience. Check in with what it feels like to be you in every way, right there on the spot. Most importantly, don't bother to describe it to yourself or do anything with it all. Just be there, with what it means to be you in that moment in the surroundings you are currently part of, sensing the world around you and inside you. By doing this you will be committing a great act of cognitive rebellion.

Trust me, when you start to do this it will become evident how lost and disoriented most people are. You will be sitting there at work or on the bus, actually feeling the seat beneath you and enjoying the ride and you will notice how caught up everyone is. How distant they seem to be, how each one is to some degree living in their own beautiful dream world. Again, this is not at all a bad quality, it is in fact part of the brilliance of being human. But it must be tempered with an understanding of the rawness of actual presence, the truth of actual reality before concepts. The truth you knew as a child, before you were told to forget it and think that everything had to "mean" something. The truth before the symbols that were taught to you.

In this way we begin to allow our own symbols to arise from the raw experience of human life, and we can build a concept of ourselves that is more based upon a true orientation to what we are. Without that, we are lost and easily manipulated. Your mind is your own, it does not belong to someone else's hierarchy of concepts. The reality of the situation is that we are all painting with the same colors, all we have to do is open our eyes and look.

CHAPTER THIRTEEN:

UNIPOLAR THINKING AND THE MYTH OF OPPOSITES

ༀ་མ་ཎི་པདྨེ་ཧཱུྃ

It is said that the truly wise are willing to live fully with the contradictions in the world. We've all heard the old adage "the truth lies in the middle". We make reference to a pendulum swinging between extremes of ideas and feelings, we have this understanding of opposites. We understand that light is the opposite of dark, we understand the mundane as an opposite to the spiritual.

We also have this somewhat mystical concept of blending the opposites. We understand the idea that there is dark within the light and light within the dark. The yin yang has a black spot on the white side, and a white spot on the black side.

This idea of opposites is a very useful tool for understanding and interacting with the world. However I am about to tell you another very big secret. A secret that has been hidden in plain sight by mystical cultures and so called "secret societies" for thousands of years. If you examine the symbols of almost any mystical tradition, this truth will become apparent. If you can get this one then you can figure out the rest mostly on your own.

The greatest secret held by wisdom culture is that opposites are in fact a frail concept, and ultimately a myth. They are a necessary part of conceptualizing the world, however limiting our view into a world of opposites is one of the primary functions of the cage we are in. Ultimately, in an absolute reality sense, opposites do not exist at all. This may be a bit difficult to believe, but there are a few different ways we can conceptualize it and actually experience it. This is the key: experiencing a lack of opposites in your conscious reality is a direct and immediate way to realize a certain portion of enlightenment.

For a conceptual understanding of this, we can see obviously that opposites define one another. There is no heads side of a coin without a tails side. There is no night without day, there is no sadness without happiness, there is no left without right, no internal experience without an external experience and on and on. This is fairly easy to grasp, but do me a favor and sit with it for a moment. Really understand that if you took away one side of an opposing set, the other side would very simply cease to exist as we know it. There is a trick in this worth paying attention to.

Now we of course want to use the idea of opposites in our lives. That is how we can tell a good and kind action from a cruel one. That is how we can work to better our lives and the lives of others around us. We have to be able to decide what is "right" and what is not. Transcending something does not mean throwing any part of it away, it means moving past it and learning to use it. I am not suggesting that we should abandon opposites as a concept. However we do not want to be used by this concept, it is a very powerful tool and it has been used against us. You should feel your world and then decide what is right and wrong yourself. Over and over and over again, without allowing anyone to force it on you.

What I am trying to tell you is that the idea of opposites is a concept that our brains create so that they can digest the world, but it is a pure illusion. A cognitive bias towards dichotomy. An illusion that is used as a trick to control us, sell us things, keep us consuming and keep us chasing the proverbial carrot, keep us believing in war. I am not sure if the powers that be are doing this on purpose, that would take a great level of wisdom. However, it is apparent that they are using this truth to keep us in check whether they realize it or not.

The idea is to swing your internal pendulum so far in one direction that before you know it you are swinging back the other way. Never getting time take a break and look at what is going on. The idea is to keep us so obsessed with opposing sides, that we never get a chance to see and accept the whole picture. They make us feel poor so that we strive to get rich, they make us feel ashamed so that we can strive for their version of perfection, they define bad actions so they can sell us their version of "good" behavior. They define beauty so that we can be told that we are ugly when we are different. They define the normal and acceptable emotional spectrum, so that we can be made to feel crazy when we defer from the norm. This programming starts at a very young age and runs very deeply.

The absolute truth of the matter is that there are no opposites at all. There are no parts at all. Negative and positive are the same thing. They need each other. That is why they attract. There is only the whole, and even that idea is odd because it assumes that there could be something other than the whole. Seeing this as part of your daily life will give you access to great and powerful inner wisdom. There is a simple cognitive trick we can use to make this work.

Take into your mind two opposites, and then allow them to sit there together without contradicting one another. You can do this by imagining any two opposites at the exact same time. Sit with the opposing sides and just let them both exist in your mind for a moment. Allow them to feel like total opposites, however also allow them to be there together. You can use any two opposites, but it is best that they truly feel like opposites. Like female and male, day and night, summer and winter, god and the devil, good and evil, friend and enemy. That type of stuff. By sitting with two sides of a whole, we can begin to experience the world around us in a direct way. We can begin to see the truth and make up our minds. If you are able to do this, you will be committing yet another great act of cognitive rebellion.

If we can learn to think in this way, it can be incredibly useful when we have a difficult decision to make in our lives. Any decision that we struggle with can make a good example here, from what to wear tonight to which college to choose. The way we usually go about it is to consider both sides, flipping between them. We dive in deeply to each side and try to figure it out. This is good, it allows us to feel each part of the whole. The problem is that we usually only switch between the ideas based upon contradiction. That is to say, we try and force each idea or side of a decision to disprove the other. We put the ideas to war in our heads, comparing them back and forth, trying to choose a side. We should do a certain amount of this, but it is only one part of the truth.

After you have had a few moments to consider your opposing sides, try this. Allow both sides of the decision to be totally real in your imagination at the same time, you can even imagine them as being on different sides. You can bring one decision in first and once you can fully imagine it, bring the other idea into your mind without dismissing the first one. Allow the opposites and the contradiction to exist in your head simultaneously and then just sit with it. Don't rush anything at all, just be with the two sides together, as one for a while. After a few moments, if you allow the two ideas to blend an answer to your decision will most likely present itself. The answer will often be some sort of fusion between the two "opposing sides", but not always. Sometimes you will see that one side is clearly preferable to the other or a third previously unseen option will present itself.

Living in this way begins to turn you into a social and conceptual renegade. It helps to disconnect you from the conceptual matrix, and can help to free your mind. You will be able to see the world as it is, instead of the way the powers that be want you to see it. You will be experiencing the raw truth as it is. You will also be experiencing unipolar thinking, which is one the primary tricks to fully waking up.

CHAPTER FOURTEEN:

PAINTING WITH THE SAME COLORS

ༀ་མ་ཎི་པ་དྨེ་ཧཱུྃ

The raw truth of the human condition is that everyone wants to be happy. The quest for happiness is what defines our lives. We may all have slightly different definitions of what that means, but overall on some deeper and more vulnerable level, we are all looking for the same things.

Everyone wants to feel accepted, connected, seen, and known. Everyone wants to have their base levels of survival taken care of while having a chance to strive for more. Everyone wants to feel safe and on the deepest level in one way or another, everyone wants to feel love and be loved. We all have this in common, each and everyone one of us. In each our own way, this desire for love, safety, exploration and fulfillment defines us. No matter how we try to hide it, we are all soft and tender. We are all a beautiful human mess inside.

If we take a real look at this idea, we can see how similar we all are. The specifics of job or partner or favorite vacation or food may vary, but at the core the drive to be alive and to seek experiences in life is the same in everyone.

Depending upon their genes, personal backgrounds and individual personalities people go after this fulfillment in all sorts of different ways, some of them quite crazy and aggressive or damaging. However, at our root, we are all working with the same desire to be fulfilled, to be loved, to be safe and to somehow feel like we belong in this world. Our actions can have very real consequences, but there is nothing inherently wrong with our internal experience. In fact it is perfect the way it is, and some very similar version of it is being shared by all of human kind.

We also tend to work with varying degrees of the same emotional responses to stimuli. Again, the particular reaction to a particular experience in a particular person may vary, but it's still all the same emotions. We all get angry, we all feel sad, we all feel lost, we all feel joy and exuberance, we all feel shame and fear, we all feel inspiration. We may be painting slightly different pictures, but we are all painting with the same colors and we are all trying to paint our own personal masterpieces. The details may change, but the overall experience is incredibly similar even when the particulars of the situation are very different. We all have the same naked base vulnerable needs, in one way or another. We are all far more similar than we are different, because we are all human.

Noticing this sameness in people comes with a great freedom to connect with others around us and a deep joy at the idea of simply being ourselves. There is nothing basically wrong with us at all, our internal experience is good and normal. Even when it is a total mess. In fact, if we use it well and with skill, our internal experience, no matter how terrible it is, can be used to connect very deeply with other people. The more deeply we have felt, the more deeply we can connect.

If we can accept our emotional experience exactly the way it is, then we can truly begin to live life as an art form. We can use this understanding of similarity to relate deeply to people. For once, we have felt deep sadness and deep joy with no resistance and no shame at all, then we can use that experience to be fully present with our friends and family when they feel great joy or sadness.

97

We can use our own internal experience to learn about ourselves and each other, in an honest way. We can use it for great good in the world, we can use it to understand the world. Because once we fully accept ourselves and see that we are all fundamentally having different versions of a very similar experience, then we can see the world in ourselves.

At that point, the real magic of daily life can begin. We can start to fall in love with what it means to truly and honestly be human.

CHAPTER FIFTEEN:

COURAGEOUS VULNERABILITY

ཨོཾ་མ་ཎི་པདྨེ་ཧཱུྃ

As we begin to become more comfortable with ourselves and our inner mechanisms, we start to relax. There is an inner tension that comes with having all of this shame programming on board, and as we begin to unravel it, we find a new exuberance for life. We actually truly begin to fully be with things and people as they are, we actually truly begin to feel where we are and be with our current experience as it is, with no judgment.

At this point, the world can begin to open up, and in some ways we find the courage to begin to act from a deep sense of honesty. At first this can feel a bit scary, because it comes along with a true sense of vulnerability to the world around us. There is a tenderness to the experience of total openness. It feels like we are being affected by everything, and that is true. That is good. Because the truth is, we are always affected by everything, and we are finally being honest about that fact.

This sense of vulnerability is an intense feeling to sit with. However if we are willing to be with it, to really look ourselves in the eyes, we begin to see the true power in vulnerability. We begin to feel the courage in it and see the true value of taking off our emotional armor and just being here. We begin to see the grace in our own mess, the raw humanness of it all. In time, the real beauty of this process starts to be obvious in the world around us. People respond to our vulnerability, they see our courage and it inspires them.

With practice, the art of being totally accepting of yourself will create a quality in you that can be felt by the people around you. This fully accepting and open quality will begin to show up in your eyes, in your body language, in the way you walk, in your voice. The way we interact with ourselves dictates the way we interact with the world, and eventually this quality of gentle and vulnerable courage will just start to roll off of you. People

100

will feel it and see it, and it will give them a sort of permission to begin to open up as well.

In this way, just by being ourselves, we can be of great benefit to the world around us and the people in our lives. Interacting with people from a sense of grounded and accepted openness has a way of cutting straight to the core. You will notice people being happily surprised by their interactions with you and they will begin to just speak and act a bit more from the heart. Your gentleness will flow into the world around you and actually make a very subtle, yet very profound positive difference. All you have to do is fully admit your own humanity and just by being there, you will begin to give people permission to do the same.

One of my favorite examples of this can be found on the dance floor of a club or a party. When we enter these situations, a lot of us are immediately faced with shame programming, I have experienced it for years. It goes like this: "Will I dance well? Do I look good? Are they all looking at me? Oh my god I look like a fool." I stand there wondering if I can even dance (which is ridiculous, because I spent several years as a pro performance martial artist and teacher. I know how to move to music). I try to start moving but my body doesn't want to do it, it's too afraid. All I can muster is a small movement in my shoulders and feet. I want to dance, but I literally feel paralyzed by my own fear of being judged.

Most of us get over this using alcohol, after a few drinks we loosen up and might begin to dance. If we keep dancing we eventually find that "zone" where it feels comfortable to be moving. Towards the end of the night we might actually start having a great time. But at some point through this process, I started to realize how silly it was. I started to notice that everyone was going through this to some degree, and honestly, no one was actually watching and judging me. They were all too busy worrying about me and everyone else judging them. The whole situation was actually entirely hysterical and kind of adorable in a way. Everyone was standing there wondering if the whole room was staring at them. No one was judging anyone but themselves.

Then something else struck me:dance floors that felt truly free usually had one key element: at least one totally unreserved, yet totally terrible dancer. You all know who I mean, that person who is out there just thrashing and smiling and dancing with no rhythm at all. Their movement is totally out of sync, but they simply don't care, they are totally free.

I started to realize that the fool dancer on the dance floor was actually the wisest person in the room and they were having the most fun. They weren't attached to the concept of dancing well, they were just fucking moving. By doing so, they were providing us all with a place to put our fear and shame outside of ourselves, they were giving us a target. But since our judgment wasn't touching them, it simply dissolved. Through accepting our judgments of them, the terrible fool dancer was literally destroying everyone's tendencies to be internally judgmental. They

102

were devouring the shame in the room and helping everyone to loosen up. Now that's Buddha AF. The key element here was a sense of I don't give a fuck joyfulness.

What I realized was that I could be that person too, and if I just let go and dance joyfully one of two things will happen. I will either look great doing it, or I will look like a fool and either outcome is a great one. On the one hand, I could dance well, have a great time and be seen looking great. On the other hand, I could look like a total fool, let go totally, and thus be in service to the dance floor and the people on it. Through a simple act of dancing however I pleased, I could summon great courage and vulnerability and help the world around me to open up. So now, whenever I can, I just fucking dance. I dance in my living room, I dance on my porch, I dance while I wait for the bus and I dance on the dance floor. It works! Sure some people just think I am crazy, but most people actually lighten up when they see me dancing out of place. They actually wake up a bit and smile.

We can do this in any social setting. Try it sometime when a room is dull, just admit to something totally ridiculous that you know we all share and see what happens. Try to do it in a way that makes fun of yourself gently or incorporates some sort of humor. That's the joy ingredient. Just totally put yourself out there. You will have to sit there for a minute and let everyone digest your courage, but most of the time it will work, and when it doesn't you can be proud of yourself for trying. It can be something totally random, like a random emotion you are

103

feeling or a fact about how you always have dirty socks. It could be something about your body or something about your mind. But whatever it is, use it as a tool to show your honest and open, joyful courage. Use it as a tool to connect and watch it change the room. Show your true loving shameless self and give people room to do the same. The effect may be subtle, but it will be present.

Showing up vulnerably and fully admitting to what we are in the moment disarms almost everyone we interact with in a beautiful way. Abandoning shame leads us to a level of courage that simply cannot be found anywhere else. Loving ourselves truly the way we are turns out to be one of the most powerful and brave things we can do. When this process takes off it's as if a light has begun to shine from within us, as if the sun is rising in our bellies and our chests.

The meek don't need to inherit the earth, they already own it.

CHAPTER SIXTEEN:

THE GREAT MYTH OF SEXUAL PURITY: UNASHAMED TO BE HUMAN UNASHAMED TO HAVE NEEDS

ༀ་མ་ཎི་པདྨེ་ཧཱུྃ

Breaking the chains of socially induced shame is a process. For some it is more complicated than others, with extra societal burdens placed on people of a specific gender, sexual orientation or people with a certain color skin. The weight of shame that is placed on us varies from person to person based upon their personal situation and upbringing, and our society is certainly not fair with the way it dishes this out. For most of us, in one way or another, this shame is very present, lurking in the background of our daily experience.

One of the primary and most delusional ways we have been taught to shame ourselves is through our sexuality. From a very young age we are taught incredibly conflicting principles regarding our sexuality. On the one hand we are surrounded by the rawness and truth of sexuality, we see it clearly in the world around us. It is present in pop culture, and through media we are taught to try and be as beautiful or strong as we can be so that we can be attractive. We are taught that being attractive and finding a mate is of paramount importance. We are taught that being straight and normative is necessary to fit into our culture.

On the other hand we are presented with the nonsense illusion of "sexual purity". We are shown monks of all sorts of religions, priests, nuns and "good people" who have thrown down the "filthiness of their sex and desire". We are taught that our desires are inherently out of control and somehow dirty, that we need to hide them and not talk about them in public. We are taught that admitting to being a sexual being is somehow "off putting" or "wrong".

This delusional and fictional ideal of sexual purity is often held up in surprising ways by surprising people.

Many (not all) Buddhists in my life for example seem offended by their own sexuality and the sexuality of others, even though they are supposedly connected to the raw state of being human. They seem to use the old "no desire" line to beat themselves up for being human. Monks swear to become as close to the fullness of humanity as possible, as close to creation as possible, while forsaking the very thing that actually creates human life.

This is in fact a very privileged and high holy stance to take, the idea that to reach purity we must forsake what we are. There is a fundamental big headed hypocrisy in it which says "someone else's impurity gifted me with this human life, which I love to have, but now I get to be pure by abandoning part of what it means to be human." Somehow, God loves human beings but hates sex. It's a fundamentally nonsensical and arrogant view. There is certainly nothing at all wrong with choosing a celibate life, for some people it is probably very healthy and the right choice, we should be what we are. For some it may even be a spiritual path. But there is certainly something wrong with holding any form of sexuality or lack of sexuality up as some necessary form of transcendence or higher mind. There is certainly something wrong and fundamentally insane about dogmatically holding celibacy or "normative sexuality" up as some example of a nonsense concept of purity. Celibacy and sexual normativity are no more a path to transcendence than sexual decadence is, they are two sides of the same coin.

107

To state otherwise is to misunderstand the very idea of transcendence itself.

Simply put, and I feel for you if this offends you, but there would be no monks or nuns to practice celibacy if two people somewhere didn't fuck. There would be no one to pray, no one to meditate and no one to pursue enlightenment. That's the unarguable truth of it, and to state that sexuality is somehow a negative or dirty thing inherently is to show a fundamental self hate and confused delusion. You ARE SEX, before you were anything at all, two people had sex. The reason you get to eat is because animals and even plants have sex in their own way.

Furthermore, if you find yourself to be obsessed with forcing people to be straight, or normative, or if you experience a lot of fear around gay or trans people, then it is probably time to take a look at your own sexuality. If the sexuality of other people is somehow offensive to you, I would suggest that you are most likely expressing a very confused and painfully illogical viewpoint on sex. I would suggest that there is a deep pain in you, a hate that has been taught to you by your elders and your religion, a hate that is distinctly not related to God or spirituality in any way. Simply put, the sexuality of others is in no way your concern or business, and if you can't seem to let go of the idea of forcing your viewpoints on others, there is a high likelihood that you yourself are not "sexually normal". The most homophobic people in the world are often gay and have been taught to hate themselves. Shaming sexuality in any way is literally insane, it is the rambling of nihilistic crazy nonsense.

People who are not highly sexual or not incredibly interested in sex are placed in a "freak" category by our society as well. They are seen by our confused sexual view as being broken somehow, as not being normal. Society wants to show us a beautiful woman wearing almost no clothes that is also somehow "chaste and clean", yet sexually available. This is clearly bullshit when we take a real look at it.

It seems that on every front we have been taught to hate our sexuality. There is nothing wrong with being celibate, there is nothing wrong with being highly sexual, there is nothing wrong with being trans or gay or straight or bi or all the other infinite possibilities for human sexuality. In fact all forms of sexual expression that are based on love are sacred. So long as your sexual expression fundamentally respects yourself and other people, then there is just simply nothing wrong or even odd about it. People are strange to the point of normal being strange, that is what it is. Anyone who tells you otherwise is attempting to project some deep seeded self hate onto you. Don't put up with that no matter who it comes from, a priest, a monk, a parent, a friend or a guru. It is crap to be discarded immediately.

We are placed into life with a very confusing teaching regarding sexuality, a fundamentally crazy way of viewing it. Holding this confused view is very painful and creates a lot of problems. This is only one of the many ways that the spiritual and moral hierarchy have failed us, and one of the reasons why people are trusting in the moral hierarchy of old less and less. Because a lot of it is simple nonsense, a lot of it just doesn't add up. Furthermore, many of the high holy people involved have proven to be human like everyone else, many of them making terrible and disgusting mistakes. Many of them using their positions as gurus or priests to prey on the people who trust them most, acting out of desperation from the position that their religion has put them in. A position of confusion and pain, a place of self hate. It would in fact be somewhat crazy and naive at this point for us not to question the spiritual and moral hierarchy at least to some degree.

There are also many ways beyond sexuality that we have been taught to shame ourselves. Most of them are, ironically, based upon the shared needs and reality of being human. Most of them are based upon our bodies and our base level emotions, things that we just have and can't really avoid having. Any small difference of skin color or race, gender or expression is jumped upon and presented as something to shame.

The thing is, when we zoom out, there is clearly no real difference between us. We are taught to shame each other because we are taught to shame ourselves, and the whole thing is crazy. The whole presentation of some perfect human being that we are supposed to be is crazy. It doesn't exist, we are all a beautiful mess and there is simply no one to hold ourselves up to, we are all in this together.

So the trick here is to seek out places where we feel shame for being simply whatever we are, and abandon it entirely. We don't even shame the shame, we see that it is a product of a response to our environment and we just sweep it out the door. Gone. This takes a bit of work, a bit of mental landscape surgery, but pretty quickly the abandonment of shame picks up momentum. We turn into shame releasing machines, noticing all of these places that we have been trained to feel bad about ourselves that just simply don't add up, places we have been taught to dislike ourselves simply for being human, lies we have been told or lies we have accidentally invented ourselves. As we realize and release our shame everyday, bit by bit we feel more free.

CHAPTER SEVENTEEN:

PERSONAL REVOLUTION
AND
GENTLE BRAVERY

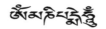

The idea of total shamelessness itself is quite profound. It can be a bit difficult to wrap our heads around at first. However when we really move past the nonsense idea that shame is a necessary part of growth, we begin to discover our inner inspiration. We begin to discover a sense of internal freedom that translates into great creativity and even sometimes joy. It turns out that all

112

locked away in our darkest places, our greatest power was waiting to be found. Like a buried treasure lost in the muck and mess of the parts that scare us.

It is said that the profound realization of enlightenment requires the ability to merge Samadhi (the sacred state of completeness within meditation) with Samsara (the endless confusion and pain of life). As we practice this profound shamelessness and embrace our inner inspiration, this idea makes perfect sense.

Through confronting our fear we discover our fearlessness. It is the act of being with fear without running that creates the power of fearlessness. In our loneliness we find one of the root causes of all love, because if we weren't lonely why would we ever seek to be with others? If we weren't lonely why would we even bother to love anybody at all? If if we never felt loss or embarrassment, if we never truly learned to cry then how would we relate to the people in our lives? How would we understand them, receive love from them or care for them? What kind of life would we have if we didn't have any ups and downs? If it was actually perfect? A very boring one, and a dishonest one if you ask me. A life without some true difficulty would be a life without art, it would be a life without the full expression of what it means to be human.

So without shame, and with a full embrace of what we truly are we can move forward into a personal revolution of sorts. We can discover our greatest power in every single part of ourselves. This is the true action and point of tantra, and of any real transcendental practice. To become what we are fully, and in that completeness, find our true power.

Out of this personal revolution comes the roaring head of what I like to call gentle bravery. Like a bright fire in the darkness, this gentle and profound strength begins to develop. Each act of emotional and total self acceptance throws wood on the fire growing within us. Gentle bravery, or true bravery, is found in the act of showing up shamelessly, fully in the present moment in a totally non aggressive way. When we do this, we have truly begun to claim the birthright of our personal power. Gentle bravery is the culmination of many acts of vulnerable courage. It grows from within every time we are fully honest with ourselves and the people around us.

Gentle bravery comes from the combination of total self acceptance, total presence of mind, personal inner inspiration and an understanding of how similar we all are. When we bring these ideas together in ourselves, when we merge them in our experience, we discover the possibility of a complete lack of aggression. We discover this deep and profound permission to be exactly what we are.

We also begin to notice subtle aggressiveness in ourselves and the people around us that we had not previously seen. This is because we have begun the process of truly accepting humanity as it is, and thus falling in love with it. We have done this through accepting ourselves, through fully loving the rawness of

114

what we are and thus discovered what is truly the same about all of us. The naked truth of being human, with no frills or moral coverings, the actuality of it. So in a way, we fall in love with the world, gently and without being pushy. Without really needing to do anything at all. We just learn to love ourselves, and the world around us the way it is.

Over time, through the practice of showing up in our lives without shame or aggression we can develop a deep sense of unconditional confidence. We gently learn to listen to our innermost voice and begin to gain the self assurance to speak and act from a place of deep self love. The more we practice trusting ourselves and our inner instincts, the more we seek to root out and release inner shame, then the more we become deeply confident.

Through a process total self acceptance we can begin to come into our personal power, the power that has been hidden from us, held down by societally induced guilt, shame and fear. Our inner compass can become incredibly strong and clear, pointing us towards thoughts and actions that truly express what what we are in our deepest personal truth. The truth that no one else can tell us, the rawness of who we each are as individuals.

The irony is that once we do this, once we truly embrace exactly what is going on, then we can actually change it. We can effect incredible change, because we are willing to work with what actually exists. While everyone else is running around yelling about what a mess their construction site is, and trying to clean it up, we are building a house. We are using the tools that being human presents us with, and so we have an edge, an honest and unarguable edge, because all of a sudden we are not afraid of ourselves anymore. This my friends, is what they (if the proverbial they even exists) are most afraid of. This is what has been hidden from us, the raw edge of true and honest, shameless and fearless, loving human experience. Once you find that, you can do almost anything.

So, we are taught shame. We are taught self hate and fear, and in that way we are taught to hate the world. We are taught to live in the future and lament the past instead of loving the present. We are taught to disengage from our senses and desperately try to control our sensory input using symbols and constructs that are not our own.

Because a world full of people who truly lived in the moment and weren't afraid of themselves or afraid of each other, a world that actually fell in love with itself and what it means to be human could accomplish anything, it would be a naturally more fair and compassionate world, a world where our small differences were seen as beautiful and perfect expressions of the same base nature of humanity. A world where we actually felt empowered to band together and fix the fixable problems that we are all faced with. A world like that wouldn't make a lot of room for division. A world like that could take care of itself.

A world like that would put a lot of powerful and oppressive people out of a job, and well, we couldn't have that. Now could we....

Chapter eighteen:

COLLECTIVE AWAKENING

ༀ་མ་ཎི་པདྨེ་ཧཱུྃ

In a world where the hierarchy has let us down in so many profound ways, we are left to trust ourselves and each other. The systems of old that have brought us to this point clearly have plenty of wisdom to share, but they are also obviously flawed in a deeply fundamental way. The social status quo and the leadership of our world is very transparently, a complete mess. The leadership of our churches and religious establishments have proven to be

117

untrustworthy and unable to truly lead the world. The leadership of our countries and local politics have proven to be manipulative and corrupt.

If we are to see our way forward through the mess that has been piled up on us by our ancestors and begin the process of truly healing this world, we are going to need to rely on each other. In each other, and in our communities, we can find one of the fastest roads to self discovery and personal awakening. But we are going to need to learn to stop turning on each other and stop turning on ourselves. We are going to need to stop trying to tune it all out and change the channel. We are going to need to be here. With it all, as it is.

By reading this book or any part of it, you have opened the door to an underground community of cognitive and spiritual evolution. A growing and all inclusive group of people who share a desire to claim their own power and change the world for the better in a fierce yet gentle way. In a dynamic, inspired and non violent way, through action in our daily lives. Each in our own way, supporting one another with our individual gifts as human beings.

At the end of this book you will find website and social media links that will connect you to this growing world of social, emotional and spiritual activists. These spaces are meant to be left open for people to collaborate on art, social justice initiatives, community organization, networking and overall connected empowerment. This network is large and active. Much of this network is based around direct action. The idea is to each fully claim our own power and then connect with deep support and understanding. In this way we may be able to begin to dramatically change this world for the better, together.

We can see how necessary it is for us to work together if we simply look at the overall function of life on earth. If you look closely, most life on this planet is single celled or close to it. Most of the vast network of life on our planet is incredibly simple: bacteria, virus, single celled organisms, all the way up to plants and even insects. Each part is moving and interacting with it's surroundings, each cell only directly and obviously impacted by the ones around it. But if we zoom out, we can see how each part affects the other. We can see one ant, and then we can see the ant hill. We can see one tree, and zooming out we see the forest. We can see how the trees all affect each other's growth patterns, how they all grow together as individuals and as one.

If we travel up the chain of the complexity of life through single celled organisms, bacteria, insects, plants and animals (and all the parts in between), we eventually end up at the most complex and self aware life on earth: human life. However, looking at our bodies, we see the same process of many parts making up a whole occurring. Each of our individual red blood cells, or liver cells, or skin cells, or brain cells are only aware of the cells that they directly interact with. Each one is on it's own personal mission, unaware of the greater whole of our bodies.

We are in fact, made up of all these little individual parts, each doing their jobs and making the whole system possible, while remaining only partially aware of the greater whole. The whole body, the "I-ness" and self identity of the whole thing can only be seen when we zoom out and see all these cells moving together. Then we see our bodies, in the same way we see an anthill or a forest. It is a collection of individual moving parts that very gracefully make up a whole.

If we were to zoom out even further, we would see the great cities of humanity, each one like a giant ant colony. We would see all the people moving around each other, unaware of anything but their surroundings, and we would see the greater whole. We would see the way we each affect each other, the way we interact to make up the bigger picture. We would see the greater face of humanity.

If we zoomed out even further we would see the whole planet, each bit of life combining to make up one whole moving organism. Each part again seemingly unaware of the larger whole, but still participating in the creation of a greater and more perfect system. If we looked closely we would see that in fact the exact same fractal math that dictates how our veins grow, how our hearts grow, and how our brain cells grow also governs the way the trees grow and branch off. The same math governs the way rivers break into smaller fingers when they flood and the way a shoreline is built by the waves. The entirety of existence is formed and created by the same laws of nature.

We would begin to see the fractal math of creation and something very clear would become apparent: There is order arising from chaos, and the exact same laws which govern the formation of all matter also govern our bodies. That is to say, we truly are a collection of simple elements, a collection of base matter. We are a conglomeration of mundane stuff, that through a process of the natural creation of order became more and more complex until it became aware of itself. We are, at our core, simply raw matter that has become aware it's own existence. Beyond a certain degree of complexity of the organization of matter which has given rise to consciousness, there is little difference between us and a glass of water, or a rock.

Given the laws of the universe, and the way matter naturally seems to constantly move towards both a more chaotic and more ordered state, we are in fact a mathematical inevitability. That's right, the laws of the universe state that you will exist, exactly as you do now. They also state that you are incredibly rare in the universe, and that the act of matter becoming conscious of itself is an amazing and precious outcome, that it takes billions upon billions of years, and can only arise under incredibly rare circumstances. Yet consciousness is still mathematically inevitable given the way matter organizes itself and the vastness of space.

So at it's base truth, you exist because you have to. The meaning of life is actually life itself. Let that free you a bit if it can. Chew on that for a moment. You are a statistical inevitability, therefore there can't actually be anything "wrong" with you at your core. You exist because you exist, you exist because you have to and you are a rare miracle of the universe. This situation has been forced on you, and you are completely at it's mercy, a gem of conscious matter in a vast and expanding universe of mundane dust. You are delicate, you are free and you are beautiful. You are meaningless and you are the meaning of life itself, of existence itself, all at once. We all are.

Imagine what could happen to the greater system if even some small critical mass of people became willing to fully accept themselves and the world around them. Imagine what could happen if we started to see ourselves as perfect little miracles connected to a greater whole. The experience of this truth, the raw feeling of it beyond conceptual understanding, is the depth of the meaning of enlightenment.

Imagine what would happen if even twenty percent of humans decided that it was actually OK to be human. That we could stop arguing over all of the small pettiness of life, we could stop hating ourselves and each other for what we are and actually treat each other with a sense of reverence. Imagine if we could find a new spirituality in that, in a pure worship of the miracle of human life, of any life at all, with no religious frills or dogmas attached.

With the current connectivity and growing technological power in the world, we could easily solve many of our global problems if we were to decide that we had the power and acted together. It really is that simple. It really is a matter of priorities. It really just takes YOU, as you are. That's the only ingredient.

We must now collectively wake up, working to move through the old conceptual reality that we have been left with, and to forge a new one, together. If we are going to have a future as a species, the way forward lies in collective cooperation and a complete abandonment of old ways of being that simply don't work. We need to stand on the shoulders of the wise before us, while utterly turning away from their failed constructs. Take what works and leave the rest behind as the rubbish of confusion that it is.

So we must start by all agreeing, as many of us as possible, on at least one thing: That life as we know it is in fact sacred and deserving of reverence outright, with no need to prove itself at all. Life deserves respect simply because it exists, it has no need to validate itself. It is validated by the fact that it is. We must learn to accept and fully love what it is to be human. We can move forward with a sense of deep respect for exactly what we are, individually and collectively. We must be willing to work with the raw, very naked truth, the direct experience of being human now, with no extra judgment or concept attached. In all of this we must be fearless, we must be fierce, and we must be gentle.

This means developing a true and deep sense of empathy, learning to really tune into what other people are feeling. The good news is that once you have truly tuned into how you are feeling in an honest way it becomes incredibly easy to tune into the experiences of others. We can network experience the way we network information, we can connect and exchange truth via empathy and compassion.

If enough of us can do this, I believe that we may begin to trigger each other and we may actually begin collectively, to wake up. I believe that this is already happening, that it is a statistical inevitability, and it is only a question of if we are able to collectively evolve before we destroy ourselves. I believe it is truly and easily possible to create a better world together. That order can rise from this chaos. I believe that the time is now, and we are the ones we have been waiting for. I believe it is why you are reading this book.

CHAPTER NINETEEN:

SPIRITUAL NINJUTSU
AND
RADICAL INTERDEPENDENCE

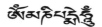

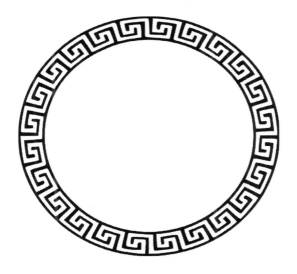

Faced with the simultaneous miracle and precipice of our current world, we have little choice but to become our own masters. There are few masters left to bow our heads to, few systems that have actually proven to be trustworthy. Sure, we can and should learn from many different people, but the concept of a moral and spiritual hierarchy is crumbling. Everywhere we look leaders are acting horrendously, setting a terrible example.

Combining this with the mess of social, political and environmental issues that we have been left with tends to put a bad taste in our mouths. For the younger adult generations today, it feels kind of like the current hierarchy has left us in a pretty bad spot. In fact sometimes it feels like they have been willing to wholeheartedly sacrifice and steal the future, our future. It is increasingly difficult to trust older people who are connected with any type of official spiritual or philosophical organization. The abuse of power and confusion at the top is just too clear. We would be crazy to ignore it.

The honest truth is, we are essentially left to clean this mess up ourselves, and none of the high holy moralism of the past is going to save us. There is no angel swooping down, no second coming. No living Buddha to show us the way. If there was, most people wouldn't be listening anyway. Holding back our curse words and making sure that we obey the rules is not going to keep the air breathable or end racism and misogyny. Being tied to shame and fear is not going to make the world a more fair and equal place. It's not going to save us. In fact, it is in part what has gotten us here.

This makes it even more difficult to stomach the preaching of our elders sometimes, because we are aware of the fact that it is their actions that have put us where are as a global society. However, it is important to remember that wisdom is still real. We can still learn quite a bit from our elders, their experiences are quite valid. In fact, they themselves had also been left to clean up the junk of generations that went before them. Many of our elders have put in great amounts of time

126

and energy attempting to create a better future. We should care for them and learn from them. We should include them where and when we can.

So it makes sense now to take what works from what the old ways have to give while turning away completely from the shaming moralism and irresponsible lack of acceptance that is also present in their teaching. Spirituality and the examination of ourselves, the examination of consciousness and our more subtle abilities is so incredibly important. I would argue that it is a basic human need. I would argue that our generations need spirituality desperately and we should not allow the failing systems of old to steal it from us. At this point, we can look to the Ninja. This sounds like a joke, but I mean it seriously. Allow me to explain.

The Ninja were essentially the jack of all trades of ancient Japan. The Ninja lived free from the normal confines of their conceptual society. They were capable of working in situations and contexts that were outside the normal bounds of Japanese societal rules of honor and hierarchy.

The way of the Ninja was simple: Do what it takes, learn what you can, abandon what does not work and only bow your head to your final goal, to your personal morals. Only bow to what you know is right. Rely on yourself, work within the illusion of the senses and above all else, do what works. Keep your word but give it rarely and with caution. Listen with an open mind. Hold to no single system of movement, thought or ideals. Learn from everything and everyone. Work free of constructs and thus construct what works.

At this point in history, it would be very helpful to adopt some form of spiritual and cognitive Ninjutsu. We are surrounded by the wisdom of the past, and if we are careful we can avoid being poisoned by it while still taking from it. Taking what works. We can let go the attachment to rebellion for the sake of it, and in so doing become truly radical. We can choose to follow our own path while still listening to the deep treasures of available wisdom. We can become what the powers that be fear the most. What they can already see coming. We can begin to evolve. Together.

What this means is being willing to explore ourselves and our true, deep hidden potential. It means being willing to believe in ourselves and practice being present, practice truly seeing what is here. I will tell you outright that after a short lifetime of spiritual exploration, meditation and tantric practice, I have expanded dramatically as a consciousness. I have discovered things about myself and the world that most people never see. I will tell you with no reservation that this quest has been, and remains to be, entirely fucking worth it.

I have found power and gentleness, joy and contentedness inside myself that is simply indescribable. The quest continues for more, to go even deeper, to wake up and be present even more. To lovingly shake the world around me and truly make a difference with the small amount of time that I get here. Every day I wake up a little bit more. We all can find this. We are born with it.

One of the first things that becomes totally apparent as we begin to relax and experience the world without concepts is the feeling of radical interdependence. When we open up and fully begin to glimpse the truth, we see that the concept of separateness itself is a myth. There is certainly some raw sense of "you" and "me" but the actual boundary lines between us are quite blurry, to the point of not really being there at all. Simply put, when you walk into a room, the color of the room itself changes subtly due to the color of your shirt and the interplay of light. Just by standing anywhere outside, you change the air flow and patterns of wind ever so slightly. When you make eye contact with another human being you are simultaneously forming memories together, thus subtly changing your personalities, at the exact same instant and in sync with one another.

The way you feel right this moment is based upon a million small factors of food in your system, your health, the events throughout your day and throughout your life, the room you are in and an endless number of other variables. Your current self is a projection of variables, an electrical signal in a brain that is subject to change at a moment's notice.

Every moment of every day our cellular structure is reworking itself in response to input from the outside world, our emotions, our thoughts, our food, our actions and a million other variables.

Every single little event affects the world around us in some way, even our hearts beating and the exchange of air in our lungs. We have power, we have an effect on our environment and we can't avoid that. We are also entirely at the mercy of our environment in every way, literally being built by it in every moment. The whole thing is happening at the same time. We are affecting the world and creating it, while it affects and creates us. There is simply nothing truly separate occurring. It is all deeply and radically interconnected. Us, the air, the rocks, the trees, other people, space, concepts and thought, all of it. Existence itself depends on all of the parts involved, it is all seamlessly interdependent.

Now I can tell you all of this intellectually and you can nod your head. You can get it on a conceptual level. Which is a good start. However, what I am talking about is practicing experiencing the world in ways that allows you to feel it. We can agree through science or philosophy or religion that we are all affecting one another and co-creating this experience. But that is different than fully experiencing the truth of no separation, or oneness. It is possible to experience this truth on such a level that you can truly become it. When that happens, very surprising and wonderful things will begin to occur in your life and in your mind.

Long before science figured out that there is no separateness and everything is relative, mystical and spiritual practitioners had figured it out on the same level of depth, to the same level of detail. Just in a different way. They had learned to feel it in their own personal experiences. They discovered incredible truths about the laws of the universe.   So much of what physicists have been discovering in recent years was documented by Hindus and Buddhists and many others thousands of years ago. Ancient people were able to discover the subtle truths of the universe without the application of modern scientific instruments. They discovered incredible truths by analyzing their own consciousness to such a degree that they found the same knowledge that scientific research has found. This is possible because we are in fact just matter, we are in fact part of the universe. The same laws that govern celestial bodies govern us, just applied in a slightly different situation.

So the literal absolute truth is present and ready to be discovered in all of us. All we have to do is dive into our own experience and explore it for what it actually is. With no limitation beyond the health and care of ourselves and others.

What I have tried to do here is share with you some more subtle truths about reality that science hasn't fully discovered yet. These truths will be discovered by science in time, just as relativity and an expanding universe were "discovered" by science almost three thousand years after they were documented by mystics in India. However, for now we are left to feel these truths inside of ourselves. This is how we evolve.

Do not allow the arrogance of the western world to tell you that something can't possibly exist simply because we are unable to detect it. This is a fundamentally flawed view, one that entirely ignores the fact that scientific research has proven to be an unfolding process. It is a fearful and control based view, that actually ignores the truth of the scientific method. Stating that something does not exist because science cannot prove that it does is both arrogant and ignorant. The truth is that time and again, scientific research has expanded upon and disproven it's own findings. The idea that subtle energies and states of mind cannot exist because they cannot be "proven" is the dogma of the scientific religion. It assumes that the current methods and tools available for gathering data are the end all be all of wisdom.

People who push the idea that something must be "proven" by science or else it is not true, are pushing yet another portion of conceptual imprisonment on you. They are actually disrespecting the scientific method itself, by applying their beliefs to the supposed objective truth. The wise and well adjusted way to phrase this would be "science hasn't been able to prove that yet so we aren't intellectually certain that it exists". People who push the idea that everything must be proven to be true forget that again and again, we have made new discoveries. They forget that again and again the truths found by mystical culture have actually proven to have incredible validity. Science is built by truth, truth is NOT built by science. Science is at the mercy of the truth, the truth is not at the mercy of science. This is a very important distinction. Science validates the truth, when it is able to using the current tools at hand.

131

In future writings I will be sharing many of the discoveries I have found, along with easy and direct ways to find them yourself via mental and cognitive practices. The techniques that I am sharing with you represent the culmination of what I have studied and experienced throughout my life as a practitioner and obsessed scholar of mystical traditions and the martial arts. What I have tried to do here is present the principle of each practice and insight, while altering the form slightly to fit our current culture.

Most of this knowledge is publicly available if you are willing to dig and know where to look. I would like to simplify this process, and present these techniques in a non religious and human based way. Because they are in fact practices to realize raw human truth. For now, I will leave you with one more cognitive and active meditation technique that can dramatically change your conceptual experience.

However, before I do, I would like to say this: If you are out there reading this book and you believe we can forge a better world together, you are not alone. If you are out there feeling this deep and inexplicable call to expand your consciousness and grow, you are not alone. If you are out there feeling the need to engage with the world and help heal it, but you feel disempowered and don't know where to start, you are not alone. There are many of us. Many of us working together and separately. Some of us are even beginning to come together fearlessly. There is a hope for the future, and there is a better world available whenever we collectively choose to stand up and create it. If you are out there reading this book, you are not alone.

So whoever you are, wherever you are, if you are reading this and you are hearing the call towards oneness and the equality of life itself, I ask you to internally stand up. Rise, in your heart right now, and know that others, somewhere are rising with you. Stand up internally and know that you can make a difference, in your own way, every single day. Stand up in your mind and know that your influence can grow. Rise in your spirit, and know that you matter. Rise up in your heart and know you are loved. Rise up in your life and make that difference, rise up in yourself and search for what is truly there, deeply hidden within you. If we all do this, together we may be able to figure this all out and find a way out of this mess, into a new a brighter future.

With that, I present to you one more very special cognitive practice, that works on a base level of human cognition.

This practice, along with all of the others presented in this book, are not mystical. Or rather, they are no more mystical than your own consciousness. There is no magic in them, and yet there is. There is the magic of human perception. The techniques I have presented are simply working with your perception and sense of self/world on a deep subconscious level. If you make it a point to practice any number of them regularly for even a short period of time, say two weeks, something strange and wonderful will begin to happen. If you even practice them a little bit you will notice a change. You will begin to have the literal sense of waking up, of brushing the crust out of your eyes. Your experience will deepen and the truth of what is actually going on around you, and within you, will begin to present itself. I hope that these techniques will provide you with a solid place to start, a solid way to begin to feel the truth. A solid way to begin to feel connected, to begin to be fully empowered. To be you, unashamed and unaggressive, fierce and gentle. Right here. Right now.

For you are exactly what the world needs and there is nothing truly wrong with you at all.

You are a miracle.

You are life itself.

~Malu

BREATH OF CONNECTION

This practice can be done just about anywhere at anytime, however it is best not to practice when you need to focus on something like driving until this type of breathing becomes natural and automatic.

You can do this at specific times throughout the day, or whenever you remember. You can do it for three breaths or for two hours. Eventually it will become part of your daily experience and that is very good. That is the goal. If it begins to feel tiring, take a break. Be gentle with yourself.

Start by breathing in slowly and feeling the breath in your nose and lungs. As you breath in, imagine you are inhaling the entire world around you. Imagine all of the parts of the room or environment you are in getting sucked in with your breath. Breathe the world in sequentially down through your body using the feeling of breathing. Start in your nose, then into your heart and lungs, then into your stomach, through the legs, and eventually your feet. Take the sensory experience of the world around you into your body with your breath, from your head to your toes.

As you breathe out, send your entire self out with it. This feels kind of like a sigh or a sneeze, but times a million. As the breath leaves your nose imagine pushing yourself out with it, out into the world. Do this with a very very slight smile. You don't even have to move your mouth into a smile, you can just feel a smile and smile with your eyes. If you can't muster a sense of happiness in that moment that is fine. But as you breath out, do it entirely and send everything you've got out into the world with your breath.

As you breathe back in again, take the whole world in again with your breath. Take what you need, take it all. Get it. Imagine it being pulled into you like a vacuum cleaner sucking up debris on the floor. Pull it all in, start by breathing into your face, then your heart and your lungs, then your stomach and then your feet.

Upon breathing out again send yourself out with the breath all over again. But this time let it become a bit more subtle, push yourself out and apply your breath to the environment you are in, but do it with a bit more of a sense of calm gentleness. Again, if you can, smile in a small and subtle way. A relaxed way. Smile in your eyes.

As you continue the practice, allow each breath in and out to become more subtle, more dynamic and gentle. Continue to breathe the entire world into your body, and breathe yourself out, but each time you breathe allow it to become just a bit more easy. With just a bit more of a light touch.

Allow this technique take time to settle in, and allow it to feel however it feels genuinely for you. If it tires you at first don't push it. The cognitive effect of this technique is powerful and can at first be a bit jarring and exhausting, even though in a way it feels great.

138

About The Movement

The Being Human Now movement is comprised of individuals working in unity to create change using direct and peaceful action in their daily lives.

Through protest organization, unified product boycotts, changes in social architecture and daily acts of courageous vulnerability; people working within the BHN network are organizing to actively create a better tomorrow. Each of us are working in our own way, bringing what we can: honestly as ourselves.

By working in unity we ARE capable of enacting real change. The tide of misogyny, racism and environmental destruction can be turned when we act together as one.

A better world is possible.

The time is now, and we are the ones we have been waiting for.

The BHN Network can be found here:

http://www.being-human-now.com/network

.

Made in the USA
Middletown, DE
04 July 2020